A History of the Grush Family of Pennsylvania and Illinois

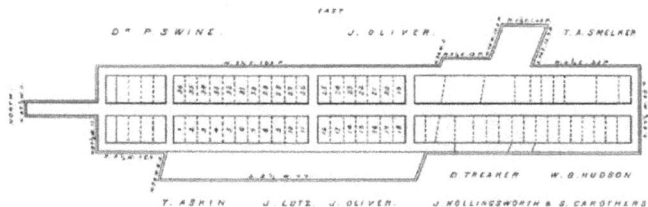

ORIGINAL PLAN OF SHIRLEYSBURG, HUNTINGDON CO., PA.
Engraved Expressly for this Work

Byron E. Grush, Jr.

A major asset in researching my family tree was familysearch.org, a massive database run by The Church of Jesus Christ of the Latter-day Saints. I wish to thank Richard Siva of Yreka, California for his kind assistant in helping me locate the Kingery Diary and related documents. Mr. Silva has painstakingly researched the Nobles Pass Trail and the history of immigration into Northern California during the 19th century. We also conferred on the diary of Adan Carlock. The curator of the Polo History Museum, Betty Obendorf, kindly and skillfully extracted obituaries of my Great Great Grandfather and my Great Grandfather from their archives, which aided me tremendously. Roger Cramer, historian of Ogle County, Illinois, and creator of a genealogical web site, communicated with me to trade historical Grush family data. Ken Ryan, a descendant of William Grush (my Great Grandfather's brother) has constructed his Ryan Family Tree and compared notes with me on several occasions. And finally, David Dahl, current owner of what was the John B. Grush farm, was kind enough to share what he knew about the house and the barn which still stands in Pine Creek Township.

——Byron Edward[8] Grush, Jr.

Historical information herein is for the most part to be considered in the public domain and may be used as source material for other uses, preferably by citing this publication. Every effort has been made to determine accuracy and cite original sources, but errors may have occurred. The author encourages new or corrected information and may be contacted at bgrush@charter.net.

Cover photo: Grush reunion, 1950s. Nordgren Studio, Polo, IL; Back cover map is from the Ogle County Atlas, Everts, Baskin & Stewart, 1872

Published in the United States by Broadhorn Publishing, Delavan, WI
ISBN: 978-0-9985454-9-3
LIBRARY OF CONGRESS CONTROL NUMBER: 2023905172

Generation No. 1

1.   JOSEPH[1] GRUSH was born in Germany in 1673 (according to Green Family Tree)

Numerous accounts of early immigration to the United States of Grushes pertinent to this line agree that their origin was France. There are two main references for this. The first is a document, "History of the Isaac Grush Family" by WILLIAM EDWARD[6] BOMBERGER (see Appendix D), in which he says:

…Huguenots, or French Protestants, were forced to leave [among them was] …a family by the name of DeGrush…who went up into Holland… until the eighteenth century when Christopher Grush came to America and settled in Moravian town (now Lititz), Pennsylvania, in 1735.

He makes no mention of a Joseph Grush and I have not found many records for him. In *Portrait and Biographical Album of Ogle County, Illinois*, Chicago, Chapman Brothers, 1886, in the biography of ISAAC[4] GRUSH (PHILIP[3], CHRISTOPHER[2], JOSEPH[1]) the writer says:

…Joseph Grush, the father of the latter [CHRISTOPHER[2]], was a native of Germany and immigrated to this country from his native land with a colony, who settled in Pennsylvania in 1745. The progenitors of the family were of French nationality and were members of the Moravian Church. They left their native country on account of religious persecution and settled in Germany. From there their descendants came to America as has been related.

A spotty record is found at http://www.mytrees.com/newanc/Germany/Born-1715/Gr/Grush-family/Joseph-Grush-ry000196-660.html which tells us:

Husband: Joseph Grush
Birth/Chris: ... 1715 at ...
Children:
    1.   Grosh, Christopher - Birth/Chris: ... 1735 at ...

Child of JOSEPH GRUSH is: CHRISTOPHER[2] GRUSH.

Generation No. 2

2.   CHRISTOPHER[2] GRUSH (JOSEPH[1]) 1711 – 1751(?)

With this generation we can find multiple references to a Christopher Grush or Grosh residing in Lancaster County, Pennsylvania in the eighteenth century. From "A Brief History of the Ranck Family" (http://groshlink.net/archives/2007/10/31/reformation-day):

…In the home of Christopher and Mary Grosh religious services were held for twenty-seven years in a large room prepared for that purpose on the second floor. The first occasion was a preaching service conducted there in 1802 by Christian Newcomer, the famed itinerant preacher from Maryland, who had been born in Bareville, Pennsylvania. Christopher Grosh himself is listed as a preacher among the United Brethren people from 1789 until his death in 1829.

Note the dates. They don't seem to work for *our* CHRISTOPHER[2].

Christopher Grosh House

There is some confusion as to whether our Christopher is the Christopher Grosh recorded in chronicles of the Moravian Church who was a minister for them in Lititz. From "The Ranks of the Rancks" (on-line edition, 10/19/2011), Ranck Family Heritage Society, Inc., http://Ranck.org. we have this:

…Christopher Grosh was born 12 January 1748 in Eichloch, Rheinhessen, Germany. On 16 March 1769, he married Anna Maria Ranck (born 25 December 1750 in Lancaster County, Pa. and died 4 January 1837). Their children were: Barbara Grosh who married Christian Hawk; Mary Grosh, 1777-1853; Catharine Grosh, 1780-1857; Margaret Grosh who married Mr. Dundore; Susanna Grosh who married Mr. Weidman; Elizabeth Grosh; Philip Grosh; David Grosh, 1776-1849; and John Grosh. Christopher Grosh died 16 April 1829 in East Earl Township Lancaster County, Pa.

Since this Christopher Grosh had a son, Philip, who would correspond to generation 3 of our line, this seems reasonable. Except that Bomberger says Christopher came to America in 1735. Bomberger goes on to say that "His wife's name, before marriage, was Kristina Elbe. They had four sons, Philip, John, David and Christopher." The Green Family Tree also shows: Kristina (Grush) Elbe 1718 -1751, Christopher Grush 1711 – 1751.

Christopher and Philip Grush are sometimes shown as GROSH in various family trees, although this family name, also with roots in Pennsylvania, is probably not related. This may have been a mistaken reading of census records. See lineage of Valentine Grosh or Grosch (Dec 1, 1767 - May 15, 1771) of Lititz, PA, in which appear a Christopher Grosh b. 1749 and son Philip b.1771 but whose marriages suggest they are different people). From "Biographical History of Lancaster County", page 242:

…In 1745 two families of the name of Grosh, emigrated to this country from Manheim, Germany. On landing at Philadelphia, two of the children were indentured as "Redemptioners," to aid in paying their passage: money. Valentine Grosh, the grandfather of the subject of this sketch, settled in East Hempfield, on wild lands…

As for emigration, in "A Collection of upwards of THIRTY THOUSAND NAMES of German, Swiss, Dutch, French and other Immigrants in Pennsylvania from 1727 to 1776" by Prof. I. Daniel Rupp, Baltimore Genealogical Publishing Co., 1965, we find the name Grosh (but not Grush or DeGrush) as follows:

…Sept 2, 1743 Foreigners imported in the ship "Loyal Judith", James Cowie-Master, from Rotterdam, last from Cowes... (on page 160 is entered the name "Valentin Grosch".) Also: Aug 8, 1764, Ship "Chance", Charles Smith-Captain, from Rotterdam - 208 passengers... (on page 356 is entered the name "Peter Grosh".)

From "Passenger Lists of Vessels Arriving in Philadelphia, 1800-1882" we find a Grosh (no first name) immigrating to Philadelphia in 1832 on the ship "Dionysus", age 50. Also, Christopher Grosh shows up in the 1820 census for Earl, Lancaster, Pennsylvania. ——familysearch.org. More confusion.

These are the only three records I have found. The Loyal Judith and the Chance transported emigrants from the Palatinate ("Der Pfalz" in German) which included the lands west of the middle part of the Rhine River (Rheinland-Pfalz). French Catholics conducted the St. Bartholemew's Day massacre in 1572 murdering hundreds of Huguenot Lutherans. The religious Thirty Years War raged on from 1619 to 1648. French Protestants fled to Germany, where conditions were almost as bad. The only safe haven for them was the Netherlands. From there they could obtain passage to the New World. William Penn had acquired part of Pennsylvania in 1681 in payment for a debt that King Charles II owed his father. He came to America on the ship "Welcome" in 1682. Penn offered his lands in Pennsylvania as a haven for the German Protestants. A small band of Krefeld Quakers and Mennonites came to Pennsylvania in 1683.There they founded the city of Germantown. They were followed by the Amish, Dunkers, Moravians, and Schwenkfelders. Grush, DeGrush, Grosh, etc., were among them. It is interesting to note that a number of Grush families settled in Massachusetts and in Maryland during this time. somehow, our CHRISTOPHER[2] ended up in Lititz, PA. (see Lititz, Appendix A)

The name, Grush, probably was shortened from DeGrush, which in turn may have been a phonetic, abbreviated, variant of de Gruchy (pronounced de Grooshi and in English-speaking communities, de Grushi). There is an extensive lineage of the family, de Gruchi in Jersey, in the British Channel Islands. The tree goes back to ca 1270, with individuals connected in one way or another back to 1089. DE GRUCHY were in Jersey from 1089. The name comes from a hamlet in the Cotentin Peninsula, the seigneurie of GROUCY near Caen, Normandy. The De Gruchys are probably descended from Hugo de Gruchy, a farmer of Jersey in 1080 under the Duke of Normandy. However, no direct linkage to the name de Gruchy for us is as yet evident.

In "Pennsylvania archives, second series", Publication date 1896, in "RETURNS AND ASSESSMENTS. COUNTY OF LANCASTER—1711" there appears the entry: Grush, Christopher............................... 2 .6. 1711? And in "Historical papers and addresses of the Lancaster County Historical Society", Publication date 1896, in a list of the German (or so-called Dutch) taxables, property-holders, etc.in Lancaster Borough, 1754, we find: John Grush, 1 lot. "Pennsylvania archives, second series, vol. xvii" mentions Grush, Christopher; Grush, Jno; and Grush, Philip. These could be from our third generation.

Before we leave the probable false lead of Valentine >> Christopher >> Philip, it is interesting to note that the second of the "two families of the name of Grosh" is a Peter Grosh. A Peter Grush, shows up in Paint Township, Somerset County, PA:

...from the PENNSYLVANIA HISTORICAL AND MUSEUM COMMISSION:
NAME: Peter Grush
OTHER: 11 May 1867 - Paint, Somerset
Pennsylvania, Land Warrants and Applications, 1733-1952
NAME: Peter Grush
CIVIL: 11 May 1867 - Somerset
Pennsylvania, Tax and Exoneration, 1768-1801

Census: 1 Aug 1860 Paint Twp, Somerset Co, Pa:
GRUSH, Peter 54 m Piren(?) Germany, farmer, $1000 of land, $234 of property
Eve 48 f Piren(?) Germany

Too young to have come on the ship "Chance" but possibly a son. Somerset County is not far from Huntingdon County where Isaac[4] settled. There were numerous Grushes there in the nineteenth century, including a Grush School and a Grush Cemetery. The cemetery:

Located in Paint Township, Somerset County, PA. From Somerset Street in Windber, take 17th Street (which turns into Railroad Street after a block) for 2.2 miles past the coal tipple. On the left side of the road is a paved access road leading into the mine area. Off to the right side of this paved road is a small clearing and then the tree line. The cemetery is located within the tree line about 100 meters up the hill and can be difficult to find.

I have spent this excessive amount of ink on the other Christopher Grosh line simply to dispel the notion that Reverend Christopher Grosh was our ancestor as he appears to be according to some versions of the Grush Family Tree that have been published. I prefer to base my version on the family history as described by WILLIAM[6] BOMBERGER, taken from his family bible:

…Christopher Grush came to America and settled in Moraviantown (now Lititz), Pennsylvania, in 1735. His wife's name, before marriage, was Kristina Elbe. They had four sons:—Philip, John, David and Christopher. Philip married a Zentmeier [Zentmeyer or Zentmyer] and settled in Pennsylvania. John married a Shafer, settlement unknown. David and Christopher never married. Philip had three sons:—Isaac, William and James. Also a daughter, Mrs. Ebey, [Eby] whose last known address was Washington, Iowa.

Children of CHRISTOPHER[2] GRUSH and Kristina Elbe b. 1718? D. 1751? (Marriage 1737?) are:
3.   i. PHILIP[3] GRUSH, b. Abt. 1780, PA. (or 1774 or possibly 1771)
       ii. JOHN GRUSH m. Unknown Shafer (?)
       iii. DAVID GRUSH
       iv. CHRISTOPHER GRUSH

Another account of Kristina Elbe gives her as b.1737- d.1780 and lists children as - Son John Grush 1761- Son Philip Grush 1776-1860 Son David Grush 1781- Son Christopher Grush 1782- Daughter Barbara Grush 1784- Daughter Catharine Grush 1786- Daughter Elizabeth Grush 1788- Daughter Margaret Grush 1790- Daughter Mary Grush 1792- Daughter Susanna Grush 1794- which makes no sense if she died in 1780.

The Eble, by the way, is a major river of central Europe, traversing Czech Republic, Bohemia, and Germany.

Generation No. 3

3. PHILIP[3] GRUSH (CHRISTOPHER[2], JOSEPH[1]) was born Abt. 1780 (or 1774 in Earl Twp., PA, d. Feb 1860, Earl Twp., PA). He married CATHERINE ZENTMYER. She was born Abt. 1783. (or 1785, d. aft 1850).

More about Philip Grush (some unverified): Philip Grush 1776-1860, Born: Lancaster, Pennsylvania, USA, Died: Lancaster, Pennsylvania, USA (?), Residence 1800 New Holland, Lancaster, Pennsylvania, 1810 Hempfield, Lancaster, Pennsylvania, United States, Marriage 1825, Lancaster, Pennsylvania, USA, Residence 1840 Bedford, Pennsylvania, United States (?), Married Catherine Zentmeyer 1783-1850.

The Pennsylvania Archives show in the county of Lancaster in 1782: Grush, John, 110 acres, 3 horses, 3 servants, taxes of 12.6 and Grush, Philip, 24 acres, 1 horse, 2 servants, and taxes of 2.18. More confusion of dates or names?

From *History of Huntingdon and Blair Counties, Pennsylvania* by J. Simpson Africa:
… The Shirleysburg Baptist Church was organized Aug. 8, 1843, with forty-nine members…. This was the earliest Baptist preaching in that immediate vicinity. The names of the original members are… Philip Grosh…

PENNSYLVANIA HISTORICAL AND MUSEUM COMMISSION lists Pennsylvania Land Warrants and Applications, 1733-1952 and gives the following information:

NAME: Stopher Grush [Christopher?]
RESIDENCE: 1779 - Earl, Lancaster
Pennsylvania, Tax and Exoneration, 1768-1801
NAME: John Grush
RESIDENCE: 1786 - Hempfield, Lancaster
Pennsylvania, Tax and Exoneration, 1768-1801
NAME: Philip Grush
RESIDENCE: 1786 - Hempfield, Lancaster
Pennsylvania, Septennial Census, 1779-1863
NAME: John Grush
RESIDENCE: 1786 - Hempfield, Lancaster
Pennsylvania, Septennial Census, 1779-1863
NAME: Philip Grush
RESIDENCE: 1786 - Hempfield, Lancaster
Pennsylvania, Septennial Census, 1779-1863
NAME: John Grush
RESIDENCE: 1814 - Antrim, Franklin
Pennsylvania, Septennial Census, 1779-1863
NAME: Philip Grush
RESIDENCE: 1814 - Antrim, Franklin
Pennsylvania, Septennial Census, 1779-1863
NAME: William Grush
BIRTH: abt 1798
RESIDENCE: 1821 - Fannett, Franklin
Pennsylvania, Septennial Census, 1779-1863
——Pennsylvania Historical & Museum Commission; Records of the Office of the Comptroller General, RG-4; Tax & Exoneration Lists, 1762-1794; Microfilm Roll: 329

[note: they seem to have moved to Franklin County by 1814. William here is probably the son of Philip[3]. Antrim Township lies along the southern edge of Franklin County, bordered to the south by Washington County in Maryland. Did they come from Maryland to Pennsylvania? Are these the same Philip, John, and William?]

More about Catherine Zentmeyer:
Descendancy for Johann Bernhard ZENTMEYER
1-Johann Bernhard ZENTMEYER b. 1 Jan 1707, Roigheim, Württemberg, Germany, d. 9 Mar 1784, Penryn, Warwick Twp., Lancaster Co., PA
+Maria Salome ROTH b. 16 Mar 1712, Bischwiller, Bas-Rhin, France, d. 1774, Penryn, Warwick Twp., Lancaster Co., PA
2-Johann Bernhard Jr.* ZENTMEYER b. 11 Mar 1740, Bischwiller, Bas-Rhin, France, d. Abt 1820, Shenandoah Co., (now Warren Co.) VA
+Catherine Susanna ZENTMEYER (born Zartman) born on December 3 1751, in Brickerville, Lancaster Co., PA.
3-Catherine ZENTMEYER b. c. 1785, PA, d. After 1850, PA
+Philip GROSH b. 1774, Earl Twp., Lancaster Co., PA, d. Feb 1860, Earl Twp., Lancaster Co., PA

Johann Bernhard Zentmeyer was a German. He was born in a small village in northeastern Württemberg called Roigheim, on the Seckach river. The church records there were destroyed in a catastrophic fire in 1719, so no birth records exist for the year 1707, however his marriage record in Bischwiller in 1739 recorded his father as 'Jacob Zentmeyer from Roigheim,' and Jacob's death was recorded in Roigheim in 1733. Additionally, there are civil records of Jacob selling wine in Roigheim for the years 1699 - 1702, as well as Jacob selling land there to Michael Vierling in 1716, and Jacob's wife Ursula died there in 1720. Bernhard's father Jacob was born in Vincenzenbronn, Bavaria in 1661. Jacob's birth record says he was the "son of

Simon Zettmair, Catholic and day labourer here, and his wife named Maria, Lutheran." Jacob's father Simon first appeared in the record obtaining a job in 1650 at a mill in Ammerndorf, Bavaria owned at the time by Johann Preuss. This mill was built in 1607 and continues to operate to this day, under the ownership of Albert Stinzendörfer, whose family has owned it since 1878.

Bernhard Zentmeyer, 45 years old, and his wife Salome 39, daughter Magdalena 3, and sons Bernhard 12, Christopher 6, and Jacob 6 months, from Bischwiller, Alsace to Pennsylvania arrived on 22 November 1752 on the ship Phoenix .

—— http://www.zentmeyergenealogy.com/germany.html

Interesting note: the 1860 census for Franklin Township, Huntingdon County, PA (the county where ISAAC[4] GRUSH came to from Lancaster) shows a number of Zentmyers, including a Major Frank Zentmyer b. 13 Sep 1836, who fought in the American Civil War in Company I, 5th Regiment, Pennsylvania Reserve Infantry (34th Volunteers rank in, Captain; rank out, Major), and was wounded and taken prisoner by the rebels at the battle of Fredericksburg, and died of his injuries, at Libby Prison, Richmond, on the 31st of December, 1862.

——Democratic Standard, Hollidaysburg, Pa., Wednesday, January 28, 1863

Child of PHILIP[3] GRUSH and CATHERINE ZENTMEYER is:
4   I.   ISAAC[4] GRUSH, b. November 13, 1802, Lancaster Co., PA, moved to Huntingdon County, then came from PA to Pine Creek Twp. in 1846. appears in 1850, 1860, 1870 and 1880 Pine Creek Twp., Ogle Co., IL census); d. March 18, 1890.
    ii. WILLIAM[4] b 1798 Earl Twp, Lancaster, Pennsylvania – d 1889 Oreana, Macon County, Illinois, m Margaret 1810 - 1878
    iii. JAMES
    iv. ELIZABETH[4] GRUSH, m. Joel Eby Jr.

More about Elizabeth Grush Eby:
Elizabeth Grush, Birth Place: PA, Birth Year: 1794, d. 1886 Piatt, Illinois, United States, Residence 1850 Buffalo, Ogle, Illinois, 1860, Nora, Jo Daviess, Illinois, United States, 1880, Oakley, Macon, Illinois, United States, Marriage Year: 1818, Leacock, Lancaster, Pennsylvania, United States, Spouse Name: Joel Eby, Birth Place: PA, Birth Year: 1793 d. 28 Mar 1861

Notes for JOEL EBY(5):
JOEL5 EBY(5) (BENJAMIN4 EBY(4), JACOB3 EBY(3), PETER2 EBY(2), DURST (THEODORUS)1 AEBI(1)) was born 06 Apr 1793 in Leacock Twp. Lancaster, Pennsylvania, and died 28 Mar 1861 in Stephenson County, Illinois. He married ELIZABETH GRUSH Abt. 1818 in Leacock Twp, Lancaster, Pennsylvania. She was born 1794 in Philadelphia, Pennsylvania, and died Abt. 1880 in Piatt County, Illinois. He died in his 73rd year and his wife in her 86th year. They had a family of eighteen children, twelve sons and six daughters. The names of the other four sons and the daughters were not given to the writer. Mostly all of the 18 children of Joel Eby's family are dead. The writer has no information concerning the descendants of the survivors.

——"The History of the Eby Family" - Ezra E. Eby - 1889 p. 112

Joel and his wife moved from Pennsylvania to the vicinity of Lena, Illinois around 1847. He continued in this area until his death in 1861. Because his children were difficult to identify, we have practically lost trace of living descendants. —— "The Genealogy of Henry Baer" by Willis N. Baer, PhD (1955)

Children of JOEL EBY and ELIZABETH[4] GRUSH:
There were 18 Including xiii. PHILLIP G. EBY(6), b. Abt. 1822, Pennsylvania; d. Aft. 1880. [who will become important in the story of ISAAC[4] GRUSH and his move to Illinois] (see Eby Family Tree in Appendix B)

More about WILLIAM[4] GRUSH:
CENSUS YEAR: 1830   STATE: PA   COUNTY: Franklin   DISTRICT: Fannet Twp
Residence —Census 1880: Whitmore, Macon, Illinois, United States
Wife: Margaret —death 7 Apr 1878, burial Union Cemetery Oreana, Macon County, Illinois, USA.
Inscription: "w/o William, m age 58y 6m 23d"

Generation No. 4

4.   ISAAC[4] GRUSH (PHILIP[3], CHRISTOPHER[2], JOSEPH[1]) was born November 13, 1802 in Lancaster Co., PA (came from PA to Pine Creek Twp. in 1846, appears in 1850, 1860, 1870 and 1880 Pine Creek Twp., Ogle Co., IL census), and died March 18, 1890. He married (1) CATHARINE BURNS 1825. She was born 1806 in PA and died 1851. He married (2) CATHERINE ANN LUTZ 1868, daughter of SAMUEL LUTZ and SARAH MEYERS. She was born November 10, 1836 in Huntingdon Co., PA, and died July 15, 1917 in Housewood Twp., Franklin Co., KS.

Notes for ISAAC GRUSH:
...Isaac Grush, a resident of Pine Creek Township and the father of John Grush, who is represented by a sketch on another page of this work, is a settler of the county of Ogle of 1846. He is a native of Lancaster Co., Pa., and was born November 13, 1802. Philip Grush, his father, was also a native of that county and was himself the son of Christopher Grush, also a native of that state. Joseph Grush, the father of the latter, was a native of Germany and emigrated to this country from his native land with a colony, who settled in Pennsylvania in 1745. The progenitors of the family were of French nationality and were members of the Moravian Church. They left their native country on account of religious persecution and settled in Germany. From there their descendants came to America as has been related. Christopher Grush was a member of the United Brethren Church and was in its ministry. The parents of Isaac Grush died in their native state. They had four children and Isaac was the youngest. He grew to manhood in the state where he was born and received a common-school education. He was married in 1825 to Catherine Burns, a native of the state of Pennsylvania and who was born in 1810.

In the spring of 1846, Mr. Grush removed to Illinois and settled on the farm on section 10 on which he is at present residing. It was in an uncultivated condition and cost him $1.50 per acre and contained 160 acres. He built a log house upon it, in which he resided with his family for 25 years. He is the owner of the original tract and also of 40 acres of timber. His wife died in 1842. [1851 is correct] By her he became the parent of 12 children, whom they named as follows: Philip, John, William, James, Mary J., Elizabeth, Emma, Catherine, Samuel, Hattie E. and Isaac. The child last named is deceased and it is supposed that James is not living. [no Samuel recorded elsewhere]

In 1868 Mr. Grush was married to Mrs. Catherine S. (Lutz) Eshleman, a native of Huntingdon Co., Pa., where she was born in 1841. [1836 is correct] She was the widow of David Eshelman, by whom she was the mother of two children: Minnie and Elsie. Virna V. [Verna] is the only issue of the second marriage. Mr. Grush is a member of the German Baptist Church. In his political connection Mr. Grush is a Republican, and in the early days of his political life was a Whig.

——Album of Ogle Co., IL, Chapman Bros., Chicago, IL Portrait and Biographical, 1886, page 477

Grandfather Isaac Grush
Born, 11-13-1802   Died. 1889

More About ISAAC GRUSH:
Burial: Pine Creek Brethren Cemetery, Pine Creek Twp., Ogle Co., IL

Obit— Death of Isaac Grush:
…Isaac Grush died at Falls City, Neb., Thursday, March 13, 1890, at the home of his son David. His remains were brought here for burial to-day. The funeral will be held at the Dunkard church, Sunday morning at 10:30. We have not learned the particulars of Mr. G's death. Isaac Grush was born Nov. 13th, 1802, in Lancaster Co., Pennsylvania, hence at the time of his death his age was 87 years and 4 months. Mr. Grush was of German extraction his ancestors settling in Pennsylvania in 1745. Mr. Grush grew to manhood and married in 1825 to Miss Catharine Burns, by whom he had thirteen children. Mrs. Grush died in 1851. In 1868 he was married a second time to Mrs. Catherine S. Eshleman, by whom he had one daughter, who resides in Nebraska. In 1846 he removed to Illinois and settled in Pine Creek, where he resided as long as he was able to continue farming. The last two or three years he has spent living with his children, mostly in the west. Isaac Grush was a most estimable citizen, modest and unassuming, honest and true. He has left to his children a heritage of honor. [Submitted by Byron Grush, transcribed by Sarah Herman]

From "History of the Isaac Grush Family" by WILLIAM EDWARD[6] BOMBERGER: (see Appendix D)

…The first mentioned son, Isaac, became the head of the Grush family, of whom we are especially interested, with a possible one-hundred-sixty-five or more living direct descendants to date, there being over three hundred names on the family tree.

His early manhood was spent in Huntingdon County, Pennsylvania. There he married his first wife Catherine. To this union were born six sons and five daughters. Philip and Isaac, twins, John, William, James and David;

10

Mary Jane who married Charles Ayers, Elizabeth, married to Josiah Bomberger, Emma, married to John Arnold, and Catherine, married to Jesse Palmatier. One daughter, Harriet, died at about thirteen years of age.

I can remember clearly of her [ELIZABETH[5] GRUSH BOMBERGER] telling about her early childhood days in Huntingdon County, Pennsylvania, and about the long drawn-out decision of the family to emigrate to Illinois, where some of their neighbors had already gone, and what an undertaking it was, especially with a large family of small means. Grandfather did not call in a truck and load all his household goods in it, load his family into a new eight-cylinder automobile, honk the horn and start for Illinois. No, he and some of the neighbors who were going with him, went to the Ohio River, not far from Pittsburg, where they built a large raft; then they brought their families and few worldly goods by wagon and loaded all on the raft, loosened the moorings and started on their long weary journey. Nothing to steer or propel the raft but pike poles in the hands of the sturdy mountaineers leaving to become prairie pioneers. For days and days they drifted with the current, aided by the pike poles. Many times they were in great danger in the rapids and swift currents, tying up at night for rest and safety. Finally they reached the great Mississippi River, where they wanted to go up-stream instead of floating. Here they hired a steamboat to pull them up to what is now Savannah, Illinois. There they were met by some old-time neighbors who had preceded them out West. They came with ox teams and wagons, loaded the goods and women and children in the wagons—the men and boys walking—and thus they started on the last lap of their long trek to the wild prairies of Illinois.

Their journey ended at a point about eight miles east of what is now Polo, Illinois, near Pine Creek. Here a log cabin was hastily erected on land that Grandfather had homesteaded. I was lucky enough to be born in this log cabin about fifteen years later.

About ISAAC[4] GRUSH and family in Huntingdon County before 1846:

Isaac may have been a cooper when he lived in or around Shirleysburg. Traditionally, a cooper is someone who makes wooden staved vessels, bound together with hoops and possessing flat ends or heads. Examples of a cooper's work include but are not limited to casks, barrels, buckets, tubs, butter churns, hogsheads, firkins, tierces, rundlets, puncheons, pipes, tuns, butts, pins and breakers. ——wikipedia.

His son John worked on a farm there in the German Valley (Philip's?). Shirleysburg is a populated place located in Huntingdon County, PA at N40.29786° W77.87416° (NAD83) and at an elevation of 597 ft MSL. Germany Valley is a valley located in Huntingdon County, PA at N40.32897° W77.84833° (NAD83) and at an elevation of 633 ft MSL. Germany Valley Cemetery is a cemetery located in Huntingdon County, PA at N40.31341° W77.84083° (NAD83) and at an elevation of 669 ft MSL.

More about German Valley:
…Dear Sir*—Your letter received. I will give you a short history of the owners of the farms in Germany Valley 64 years ago or in the year 1845. Beginning at the old fallen mill, south of the old stone church: John Young, Philip Grush, …These persons all lived at the old fullen mill.
——Letters, C. B. Smelker to Mr. Chas. H. Welch, around 1909, "History of Mount Union, Shirleysburg and Shirley Township" by Welch, Charles Howard, b. 1880 (see Appendix C)
[this is probably PHILIP[5] GRUSH, b. January 09, 1826, as there is no record of Isaac's father having moved to Huntingdon County and no Grush burials recorded in the German Valley Cemetery.]

The Germany Valley Dunkard Church

THE EARLY DUNKARD CHURCH

...What is known as the Aughwick Church of the Brethren, or Dunkard, was organized about 1802. The flock at first was small, numbering about six. These pioneer worshippers were faithful and devout, and as a rule were strict in the performance of their religious obligations. Prior to the day of churches they worshiped -out under the trees and in barns, or in any convenient place where the Gospel might be preached. ...These people spoke German, being unfamiliar with English, hence for a while progress was slow. Later Jacob Lutz [his granddaughter was Catherine S. (Eshelman) (Lutz) Grush, Isaac's second wife] was chosen as the minister, and he being able to speak English fluently. a little more progress was made...

——"History of Mount Union, Shirleysburg and Shirley Township" by Welch, Charles Howard
(see Appendix F, The Lovefeast)

More About CATHARINE BURNS:

Catherine BURNS was born 08 JUN 1806 in Huntingdon Co., PA, and died 14 OCT 1851 in Polo, Ogle Co., IL. She married Isaac GRUSH ABT 1825 in Lancaster Co., PA. He was born 13 NOV 1802 in New Holland, Lancaster Co., PA, and died 13 MAR 1890 in Pine Creek, Ogle Co., IL.

Her parents were Isaac BURNS, Death: in Shirleysburg, Huntingdon Co., PA, and Catherine LATTA b: ABT 1778 in Huntingdon Co., PA, Death: ABT 1864 in Dresden, Poweshiek Co., IA, Married: ABT 1795 in Huntingdon Co., PA

More about Isaac Burns: The pioneer wheelwrights of Shirleysburg were Isaac Burns, whose shop was between the old John Cooper's tavern and store and Sharrar's cabinet-shop... (from History of Huntingdon and Blair Counties, Pennsylvania by J. Simpson Africa Philadelphia, PA: Louis H. Everts, 1883) According to his granddaughter Mary Jane Grush's obit he was a solder in the Revolutionary War. (see Latta Genealogy, Appendix E)

Children of Catherine LATTA and Isaac BURNS are:
i.   Isaac BURNS was born in Huntingdon Co., PA. Married: ABT 1795 in Huntingdon Co., PA
ii.   Jane BURNS was born in Huntingdon Co., PA. She married Unknown CRANE.
iii.   Sarah BURNS was born 26 AUG 1796 in Huntingdon Co., PA, and died 25 MAR 1799 in Huntingdon Co., PA.
iv.   Nancy BURNS was born 06 APR 1799 in Huntingdon Co., PA.
v.   James BURNS was born 04 NOV 1800 in Huntingdon Co., PA.

vi.   Mary BURNS was born 28 AUG 1802 in Huntingdon Co., PA. She married Morgan CORNELIUS ABT 1823 in Shirley Twp., Huntingdon Co., PA, son of Peter CORNELIUS and Rebecca MORGAN. He was born ABT 1798 in Huntingdon Co., PA, and died BEF 1870 in Deep River Twp., Poweshiek Co., IA.

vii.   Amelia BURNS was born 07 JUN 1804 in Huntingdon Co., PA, and died 12 APR 1857 in Polo, Ogle Co., IL. She married Lewis CORNELIUS ABT 1826 in Huntingdon Co., PA, son of Peter CORNELIUS and Rebecca MORGAN. He was born 27 DEC 1797 in Shirley Twp., Huntingdon Co., PA, and died 25 APR 1881 in Buffalo, Ogle Co., IL. Burial: Pine Creek Brethren Cemetery, Pine Creek Twp., Ogle Co., IL

viii.   Catherine BURNS was born 08 JUN 1806 in Huntingdon Co., PA, and died 14 OCT 1851 in Polo, Ogle Co., IL. She married Isaac GRUSH ABT 1825 in Lancaster Co., PA. He was born 13 NOV 1802 in New Holland, Lancaster Co., PA, and died 13 MAR 1890 in Pine Creek, Ogle Co., IL. Burial: Pine Creek Brethren Cemetery, Pine Creek Twp., Ogle Co., IL

ix.   Sarah BURNS was born 06 JUL 1809 in Huntingdon Co., PA, and died BEF 1860 in Martinsburg, Blair Co., PA. She married Daniel O. MYERS ABT 1830 in Huntingdon Co., PA. He was born ABT 1801 in MD.

x.   John BURNS was born ABT 1816 in Huntingdon Co., PA, and died BEF 1880 in Dresden, Poweshiek Co., IA. He married Elizabeth UNKNOWN ABT 1839 in Huntingdon Co., PA. She was born ABT 1816 in PA.

More about Lewis Cornelius, 1797 – 1881:
Lewis Cornelius was born on month day 1797, in birthplace, Pennsylvania, to Peter Cornelius and Rebecca Cornelius (born Morgan). Husband of Amelia (Burns) Cornelius. Father of Richard Scott Cornelius, Rebecca Jane Cornelius, John Burns Cornelius, James Cornelius, Samuel D. Cornelius, Elias Cornelius and Silas Cornelius.

More about the journey of the Isaac Grush Family from Pennsylvania to Illinois:

Sometime before 1846, Philip Eby (son of Joel Eby and ELIZABETH[4] GRUSH) wrote a letter to his uncle, WiILLIAM[4] GRUSH (PHILIP[3], CHRISTOPHER[2], JOSEPH[1]) describing land opportunities in Illinois. (see Appendix H) He says that "Uncle Isaac Grush is going to move with us to Rock River Settlement. ...There is a hundred familys going to from Washington County Maryland. I would like to see you and the family come out next summer to Ogle County Illinois that is the place that we are going to. Isac is going to the same neighborhood. ... I started from Illinois for home on the 20 day of October and landed on the 11 of November. I came by water all the way home."

In 1846, Isaac took his family, wife Catherine, children Philip (age 20), John (age 18), William (age 17), James (age 14), Mary Jane (age 12), Elizabeth (age 10), Emma (age 6), and Catherine (age 4) by wagon to the Ohio River, not far from Pittsburg, where, with some other families, built a large raft. They preceded down the Ohio River to the Mississippi River where they were towed up to Savannah, Illinois. They were met there by Sammy Funk who transported them to Pine Creek Township near Polo, Illinois. (see Appendix D, History of the Isaac Grush Family) In 2012, intrigued by this story and trying to imagine what a journey such as this would have been like, I wrote a novel of historical fiction (note the word "fiction") entitled *All the Way by Water*, ISBN-13: 978-0615720715 (Broadhorn Publishing), in which I dramatized the trip, taking a few liberties with truth unknown. I placed the family on a flatboat instead of a raft and called them "Grosh" in order to distance myself from reality for penning an adventure.

Children of ISAAC[4] GRUSH and CATHARINE BURNS are:

    i.   PHILIP GRUSH, b. January 09, 1826, Huntingdon Co., PA (appears in 1850 Pine Creek Twp., Ogle Co. and 1860 Lima Twp., Carroll Co., IL census); d. January 14, 1890, Lanark, Rock Creek Twp., Carroll Co., IL. (a twin)

    ii.   ISAAC GRUSH, b. January 09, 1826, Huntingdon Co., PA. (a twin, died very young)

    iii.   JOHN B. GRUSH, b. September 22, 1827, Huntington Co., PA (appears in 1870, 1880 and 1900 Pine Creek Twp., Ogle Co., IL census); d. May 22, 1906, Stratford, Ogle Co., IL.

    iv.   WILLIAM GRUSH, b. November 20, 1829, Huntingdon Co., PA (appears in 1860 Pine Creek Twp., Ogle Co., IL census); d. May 06, 1902.

    v.   JAMES GRUSH, b. Abt. 1832, Huntingdon Co., PA.

    vi.   MARY JANE GRUSH, b. March 07, 1834, Huntingdon Co., PA (appears in 1900, 1910 and 1920 Woosung Twp., Ogle Co., IL census); d. April 27, 1924, Woosung Twp., Ogle Co., IL.

    vii.   ELIZABETH GRUSH, b. May 03, 1836, Huntingdon Co., PA; d. February 07, 1913, Gowrie, Webster Co., IA.

    viii.   EMMA GRUSH, b. June 17, 1840, Huntingdon Co., PA; d. April 03, 1929, Freeport, Stephenson Co., IL.

    ix.   CATHERINE GRUSH, b. August 15, 1842, Huntingdon Co., PA; d. July 15, 1936; m. JESSE PALMATIER; b. August 08, 1830; d. February 04, 1918.

        More About CATHERINE GRUSH:
        Burial: Sixteen Cemetery, Thornburg, Keokuk Co., IA

        More About JESSE PALMATIER:
        Burial: Sixteen Cemetery, Thornburg, Keokuk Co., IA

    x.   HARRIET "HATTIE" GRUSH, b. August 13, 1846, Ogle Co., IL; d. February 17, 1860.

        More about Hattie Emma Grush: The marriage of Peter Horner and Wilhelmina Biesecker Horner was blessed with five children: 1. William Edmund Horner, born May 30, 1861, married Hattie Emma Grush on December 10, 1885, in Polo, Ogle County, Illinois and died January 10, 1940. This couple had 3 children.

    xi.   DAVID ROLAND GRUSH, b. August 05, 1850, Ogle Co., IL (appears in 1880 Pine Creek Twp., Ogle Co., IL and 1900 Falls City, Richardson Co., NE census); d. February 11, 1928, Falls City, Richardson Co., NE.

NOTE: One other possible child is Sarah Ann Grush, 1837 - 1929
Sarah Ann Grush was born on month day 1837, at birthplace, Pennsylvania, to Isaac Grush and Catherine Grush (born Burns) as per Ken Ryan. Ryan has her buried in Pine Creek Brethren Cemetery in Illinois in 1940 – apparently Sarah passed away on April 3 1929, at age 92 in Freeport, Stephenson, Illinois, United States. Records on Sarah Ann Grush supplied him by Jean Deets, 1302 E. 14th St., Sterling, IL 61081-2639. This record places Shirleysburg in Lancaster County, Pennsylvania (it is in Huntingdon Co.). Another Sarah Ann Grush record exists for Sarah Ann (Grush) Ridenour 1808 – 1881 (parents Heinrich Grosh, JR and Elizabeth Ranck), also Sarah Ann Reitenauer/Ridenour/Ritenour (born Grush), 1811 – 1881.

Child of ISAAC GRUSH and CATHERINE LUTZ is:

    xii.   VERNIE Z. GRUSH, b. October 20, 1869, IL; d. March 10, 1954; m. FRANK SHERMAN WAGNER, January 01, 1889, Richardson Co., NE; b. March 21, 1865, Ogle Co., IL (living in Baker Twp., Gove Co., KS in 1900); d. October 15, 1944.

Vernie Z. Grush married Frank S. Wagner, son of John A. Wagner and Mary Stover, on 1 January 1889; No children. ——George F. P. Wanger, A Genealogy of the Descendants of Rev. Jacob Price, 595

More about Catherine S. (Eshelman) (Lutz) Grush:
Born November 13, 1836, in Pennsylvania, United States
Died 1917 in Black Hawk County, Iowa, USA
Child of Catherine Eshelman Lutz Grush is Anna Eshelman (?)
...possibly born Lutz, married David Deahl Eshelman b. (September 29, 1832 Woodbury, Bedford, Pennsylvania, Died September 15, 1864 in Shirleysburg, Huntingdon, Pennsylvania) in 1860, children of David and Catherine being Minnie May Eshelman, b June 15, 1862, and Anna Alsamena Eshelman, b. April 2, 1864] David was Son of John Eshleman, Rev. and Susan Deahl and Husband of Susan Brumbaugh and Catharine A. Lutz, also with Susan was Father of Mary Susan Eshelman, b. March 19, 1858.
Catherine Lutz was one of seven children of Samuel M. Lutz (b. 1805 d. 1875) and Sara F. Myers (m. 1828).
Samuel Lutz was the son of Jacob Lutz (b. 1763 d. 1826) married Catharine Long (b. 1767 d. 1854) in 1788.

from David S. Lutz, Charlottesville VA <DLutz22901@aol.com> 15 Nov 2005:
...In Germany Valley in an abandoned cemetery is a gravestone which reads:

Jacob Lutz
died July 29, 1826
Aged 62 yrs 8 mo. 8 days

Jacob's wife, Catherine Long, was born & raised in the Manheim area of Lancaster County, PA. I did locate a "Jacob Lutz" who was in the Lancaster County militia in 1781. Jacob's father-in-law, Joseph Long, was from Lancaster County. Both Jacob and Joseph sold their PA farms in 1787 and moved to Maryland where they farmed adjoining farms. In 1795, they sold their MD properties and moved to Germany Valley where they, again, farmed adjoining farms.

Jacob Lutz (b. 1763 d. 1826) married Catharine Long (b.
1767 d. 1854) in 1788 (month & day unknown). They had ten children:
8. Samuel M. (b. 1805 d. 1875) m. Sara F. Myers
Samuel M. Lutz who married Sara F. Myers in 1828 and had
seven children:
4. Catherine (b. 1836 d. 1917) m. Isaac Grush

...In 1868 Mr Grush was married to Mrs. Catherine S. (Lutz) Eshleman, a native of Huntingdon Co., Pa., where she was born in 1841. (1836 is correct) She was the widow of David Eshelman, by whom she was the mother of two children: Minnie and Elsie. Virna V. (Verna) is the only issue of the second marriage. Mr. Grush is a member of the German Baptist Church. In his political connection Mr. Grush is a Republican, and in the early days of his political life was a Whig.
    ——Portrait and Biographical Album of Ogle Co., IL, Chapman Bros., Chicago, IL, 1886, page 477

About David Eshleman:
David Eshleman and myself constituted a class of three in surveying. We all mastered the science so far as the books were concerned. I never did much practical surveying except to lay out lots after I came to Roaring Spring. Mr. Eshleman did some surveying, but he accidentally had part of his hand torn off in a threshing machine, and died of lock-jaw pretty early in life.
    ——"Looking Eighty Years Backward And A History of Roaring Spring", Pa. by D. M. Bare

David Deahl ESHLEMAN was born on 29 September 1832 at near in Woodbury, Bedford Co., PA. He died on 15 September 1864 at the age of 31 in Shirleysburg, Huntingdon Co., PA. He was buried at near the Germany Valley Meeting House in Huntingdon Co., PA.3948 David was a member of the German Baptist Brethren Church. Parents: Rev. John ESHLEMAN-136595 and Susan DEAHL.
Spouse: Susan BRUMBAUGH. Susan BRUMBAUGH and David Deahl ESHLEMAN were married on 6 January 1857. Children were: Mary Susan ESHLEMAN.

Spouse: Catharine A. LUTZ. Catharine A. LUTZ and David Deahl ESHLEMAN were married. Children were: Minnie May ESHLEMAN, Anna Alsamena ESHLEMAN.

——http://freepages.genealogy.rootsweb.ancestry.com/~jdavis/b1171.htm

Generation No. 5

5.   PHILIP[5] GRUSH (ISAAC[4], PHILIP[3], CHRISTOPHER[2], JOSEPH[1]) was born January 09,1826 in Huntingdon Co., PA (appears in 1850 Pine Creek Twp., Ogle Co., IL census), and died January 14,1890 in Lanark, Rock Creek Twp., Carroll Co., IL. He married CATHERINE BINGAMAN April 05,1849 in Ogle Co., IL, daughter of GEORGE BINGAMAN and MARGARET SARBER. She was born February 10,1828 in Lower Mahanoy Twp., Northumberland Co., PA, and died September 22,1928 in Chicago, Cook Co., IL.

Philip Grush was born 4, 5 9 Jan 1826 in Shirleysburg, Huntingdon, Pennsylvania, USA. He died 14 Jan 1890 in Lanark, Carroll, Illinois, USA. Philip married Catharine Bingaman on 5 Apr 1849 in Ogle, Illinois, USA. Philip resided 1860 in Lima, Carroll, Illinois. He resided 1880 in Lanark, Carroll, Illinois, United States. The 1850 census shows him to have been a school teacher.

Catharine Bingaman was born 10 Feb 1828 in Lower Mahanoy, Northumberland, Pennsylvania, USA. She died 22 Sep 1928 in Chicago, Cook, Illinois, USA. Catharine married Philip Grush on 5 Apr 1849 in Ogle, Illinois, USA. Catharine resided 1900 in Chicago Ward 12, Cook, Illinois. She resided 1920 in Chicago Ward 13, Cook (Chicago), Illinois. She resided 1860 in Lima, Carroll, Illinois.

John George Bingaman [Parents] was born 11 Nov 1803 in Lower Mahanoy, Northumberland, Pennsylvania, USA. He died 19 Oct 1847 in Union Grove, Whiteside, Illinois, USA and was buried 1847 in Buffalo, Ogle, Illinois, USA. John married Margaret Sarber.

Margaret Sarber was born 2 Jun 1803 in Pennsylvania, USA. She died 31 Jul 1884 in Ogle, Illinois, USA and was buried 1884 in Buffalo, Ogle, Illinois, USA. Margaret married John George Bingaman. Margaret resided 1850 in Lima, Carroll, Illinois. She resided 1880 in Lima, Carroll, Illinois, United States.

Children of PHILIP[5] GRUSH and CATHERINE BINGAMAN are:
  i.   ISAAC[6] GRUSH, b. Abt. 1850, Pine Creek Twp., Ogle Co., IL; d. October 04, 1931.
       More About ISAAC NEWTON GRUSH:
       Burial: Oxford Cemetery, Oxford, Harlan Co., NE

  ii. MARY GRUSH, b. Abt. 1853, Pine Creek Twp., Ogle Co., IL ; d. December 03, 1941; m. RICHARD BRACKIN; b. 1869; d. 1932.
  iii. JOHN HENRY GRUSH, b. February 28, 1856, Pine Creek Twp., Ogle Co., IL; d. January 14, 1926.
       More About JOHN HENRY GRUSH:
       Burial: Elm Grove Cemetery, Washington, Washington Co., IA

       John Henry Grush was born 19 Feb 1856 in Grove City, Jasper, Illinois, USA. He died 14 Jan 1926 in Muscatine, Iowa, USA. John married Mattie Dayton on 1876 in , Washington, Iowa, USA. John resided 1910 in Washington Ward 1, Washington, Iowa. He resided 1885 in East River. He resided 1880 in East River, Page, Iowa, United States. He resided 1910 in Washington, Wapello, Iowa.

Mattie Dayton was born 4, 5 1856 in Page, Iowa, USA. She died 7 Nov 1932 in Chicago, Cook, Illinois. Mattie married John Henry Grush on 1876 in Washington, Iowa, USA. Mattie resided 1930 in Chicago, Cook, Illinois. She resided Jan 1925 in Muscatine Ward 3.

    iv.   ANNA GRUSH, b. Abt. 1859, Pine Creek Twp., Ogle Co., IL.

    v.   SARAH GRUSH, b. January 07, 1860, Carroll Co., IL; d. August 21, 1947, Chicago, Cook Co., IL; m. JOHN F. KLOEPPING.

Notes for SARAH GRUSH:
Illinois Deaths and Stillbirths Index, 1916-1947

Name: Sarah Grush Kleppin
Birth Date: 7 Jan 1860
Birth Place: Lanark, Illinois
Death Date: 21 Aug 1947
Death Place: Chicago, Cook, Illinois
Burial Date: 23 Aug 1947
Burial Place: Lanark, Carroll, Illinois
Cemetery Name: Local
Death Age: 87
Occupation: Housewife
Race: White
Marital Status: W
Gender: Female
Residence: Chicago, Cook, Illinois
Father Name: Phillip Grush
Father Birth Place: Penn
Mother Name: Catherine Bingaman
Mother Birth Place: Penn
Spouse Name: John F.

More About SARAH GRUSH:
Burial: Lanark Cemetery, Lanark, Rock Creek Twp., Carroll Co., IL

    vi.   JAMES E. GRUSH, b. October 1861, IL (appears in 1900 Brookville Twp., Ogle Co., IL census, moved to KS). (Wichita, Sedgwick Co., KS) (MARRIED Margaret E Fager 26 DEC 1886, Ogle Co., IL) James Edward Grush was born 19 Oct 1862 in Lanark, Carroll, Illinois, USA. He married Maggie E Fager. James resided 1880 in Lanark, Carroll, Illinois, United States. He resided 1930 in Valverde, Sumner, Kansas. He resided 10 1900 in Brookville, Ogle, Illinois, USA.

Maggie E Fager was born 1861 in Brookville, Ogle, Illinois, USA. She married James Edward Grush.

    v.   Della Irene Grush was born 23 Aug 1868 in Lanark, Carroll, Illinois, USA. She died Feb 1899 in Chicago, Cook, Illinois, USA. Della resided 1880 in Lanark, Carroll, Illinois, United States.

5. JOHN B.[5] GRUSH (ISAAC[4], PHILIP[3], CHRISTOPHER[2], JOSEPH[1]) was born September 22, 1827 in Huntington Co., PA (appears in 1870, 1880 and 1900 Pine Creek Twp., Ogle Co., IL census), and died May 22, 1906. He married (1) MARY JANE TENNIS May 23,1861 in Ogle Co., IL. She was born December 08, 1835, in IN, and died February 23, 1870. He married (2) ANNIE LEE August 31, 1872, daughter of STEPHEN LEE and ELIZA HOUCK. She was born January 1837 in Frankford, Herkimer Co., NY.

More about Mary Jane Tennis:
Note: Ancestry.com OneWorldTree shows Mary J Tennis to be born in Ogle County. Illinois but the 1850 US Census for Henry County. Illinois shows her born in Indiana. Father: William Tennis b: ABT 1804 in Pennsylvania. Mother: Delila Unknown D: ABT 1806 in Virginia. Burial: Pine Creek Brethren Cemetery. Pine Creek Township. Ogle County. Illinois.
——The Horner Family Of Carroll County, Illinois (And Nearly Everyone Else)

Children of William Tennis and Delila Unknown are: Catherine Tennis, b. Abt. 1833 (married WILLIAM[5] GRUSH), Indiana, Mary Jane Tennis, b. Dec 1835, Indiana, d. 23 Feb 1870, Ogle County, Illinois, Sarah Tennis, b. Abt. 1838, Indiana, Susannah Tennis, b. Abt. 1842, Indiana, Delila E Tennis, b. Abt. 1845, Indiana, William W Tennis, b. Abt. 1846, Indiana, Thomas Tennis, b. Abt. 1853, Illinois.

More about Annie Lee Berger Grush:
Annie Lee and William W. Berger were married Sept. 4, 1862, at Milton, Rock County, Wis., and returned to Ogle County, where they passed the ensuing winter. In the spring of the next year Mr. Berger went to Pike's Peak with a company, and started from there for New Mexico, and was killed by the marauding Indians on the plains. The bereaved wife returned to Wisconsin, where her son was born in Janesville, Rock County, Aug. 8, 1863. She was still living there when she was married to Mr. John Grush, of Pine Creek Township. Moved with son, Charles Berger (see Appendix N) to Rockford, Illinois, shortly after husband John Grush's death in 1906. She died Sept,1907, in Rockford, Illinois. Burial Oakville Cemetery in Janesville, Wisconsin.

More About JOHN B. GRUSH:
Burial: Pine Creek Brethren Cemetery, Pine Creek Twp., Ogle Co., IL (see Appendix G, Pine Creek Cemetery)

Obit:
Death of John Grush
After a long illness John Grush died at his home in Stratford, Tuesday evening, May 22, 1906 at 6 o'clock. John Grush was born in Huntington County, Pennsylvania, in 1827 and in 1846 he came west with his parents. They came by boat down the Ohio river and then up the Mississippi to Savanna, then traveled over land on wagons to Pine Creek, Illinois. In 1852, Mr. Grush was one of a company of men who took their ox teams and journeyed to California and while there he spent most of his time mining. In 1860 he returned to Ogle County, Illinois. In 1862 he was united in marriage with Miss Mary Tennice [Tennis] of Eagle Point. To this union were born two daughters and one son. In 1870 this union was broken by the death of his wife and in the fall of 1871 he was again united in marriage with Mrs. Anna Burger [Berger], and to this union was born a son, who died in 1899. Mr. Grush was a kind husband, a good neighbor and a devout Christian, being a member of the United Brethren church. Mr. Grush was of a family of twelve children of whom remain to mourn his death. D.R. Grush of Falls City Nebraska; Mrs. Emma Arnold of Freeport; Mrs. Elizabeth Bumbiger [Bomberger] of Gowrie, Iowa; Mrs. Catherine Parmatier [Palmatier] of Thornsburg, Iowa and Mrs. Mary J. Ayres of Polo. The funeral services were held Thursday afternoon at three o'clock at the Pine Creek Brethren church. Rev. Circle officiating. Interment was made in the Pine Creek cemetery. Near relatives from a distance who were present at the funeral were D.R. Grush and three sons, William, Elmer and Jesse, of Falls City Nebraska; Mrs. Mary Price of Albion, Iowa; John Arnold and wife, Dr. R. A. Arnold and wife of Freeport, Edward Horner and family of Lanark, Chas. Burger of Rockford and Alex Grush of Naperville. [Submitted by Byron Grush, transcribed by Kris Dunlap]

Biography:

John B. Grush is a prominent citizen of the township of Pine Creek, where he located in 1846 when he was 18 years of age. In that year his parents removed to Ogle County, and settled in the same township in which the son is now the representative of an honored name. Mr. Grush was born in Huntington Co., Pa., and is the son of Isaac Grush, the date of his birth being Oct 21, 1828. He was 18 years old when, in 1846, he accompanied his father's family to Ogle County. Previous to the change which the removal made in his circumstances, he was employed on a farm two years. He was occupied as a farm laborer four years after coming hither, and through two summers managed a breaking team.

In the spring of 1852, he started for California. He made the journey there overland and arrived at Shasta City Aug. 26th of the same year in which he set out for that land of golden promise. He passed about 14 months in the capacity of a miner, and then became interested in the business of a packer. The train which he conducted consisted of about 50 mules, and the work embraced in the vocation included the sending of supplies to miners and others beyond the reach of the regular traders in the shops and the markets. He remained in California until1860 when he returned via the Isthmus, to New York. The trip consumed 26 days, through four of which they were almost overwhelmed by a storm on the Pacific.

In the spring of 1861, he bought the farm on which he is at present prosecuting his business plans May 23, 1861, his marriage to Mary J. Tennis took place. She was born in 1836, in Indiana. The issue of this union were three children, named Ida May, Hat-tie E. and Alexander J. The mother died Feb. 23, 1870. The second marriage of Mr. Grush took place Aug. 31, 1872, Mrs. Annie (Lee) Berger becoming his wife at that date. She was born in Frankford, Herkimer Co., N.Y. and is the daughter of Stephen and Eliza (Houck) Lee. Her parents were natives of the same county in which she was born. Their family emigrated to Magnolia, Rock Co., Wis., in 1851, where her father and mother died. Her first husband, William Berger, to whom she was married Sept. 4, 1862, went across the plains to Pike's Peak, and was killed by the Indians. By him she had one child, Charles B. There is one child by the second marriage, Otto J.

With the exception of a period of two years, which he passed in Polo, Mr. Grush has been interested farming. His landed estate consists of 240 acres land, all of which is in an advanced state of cultivation. The residence on the place is good and suitable, and the barn on the farm, which was built in 1868, is one of the best in the township. It is 44 x 68 feel in dimensions, and has a basement, costing in construction $1,8oo.

Mr. Grush is a member of the United Brethren Church, and his wife belongs to the Methodist denomination. In political connection he is a Republican of sound and substantial views. He has held various township offices, and is well and widely known for his hospitable and generous spirit.

———Portrait and Biographical Album of Ogle County, Illinois, Chicago, Chapman Brothers, 1886

John Grush farm, Ogle County Atlas, Everts, Baskin & Stewart, 1872

The barn still stands, near the corner of Lowell and Judson, Pine Creek Township

More about John B. Grush going to the California gold rush in 1852:

The Beinecke Rare Book & Manuscript Library at Yale University in New Haven, CT contains a manuscript entitled, "Solomon Kingery's Trip to California in 1852". Kingery, born 1831 in Dauphin County, PA (Father: Daniel Kingery Gingrich b. 19 Oct 1805 in Dauphin County, Pa. Mother: Susanna Ryder Hoover), lived at the time in Pine Creek Township in Ogle County, IL. Together with a number of other Pine Creekers, including JOHN[5] B. GRUSH and JAMES[5] GRUSH, he journeyed by wagon train to Shasta City, CA arriving on 08/22/1852. The manuscript consists of diary-like letters he sent home to his parents. The routes taken were Pine Creek to Council Bluffs, Omaha, Platte River East of Ft. Laramie on the north side, Child's Cutoff, Sublette Cutoff (also Kinney, Slate Creek and Dempsey-Hockaday Cutoffs), Hudspeth Cutoff, Applegate Trail to Goose Lake, and Nobles Road. They were apparently the first, or at least one of the first wagon trains to use the Nobles Pass over the mountains. Others in the party, mentioned by Kingery in his letters, included William H Sadler (or Saddler), Nelson Tice (who died and was buried along the way), Mr. Harris, Mr. Biggins, Mr. Hoisington, and Mr. and Mrs. Freet and child.

Notes for Nelson Tice:
Poor Nelson Tice never reached the golden state. He died and was buried in a quiet spot along the trail where his grave was observed by Zarah McClung who also traveled to California by wagon in 1852.

There are historical markers placed now along the Immigrate Trail. Along the Nobels Trail two of them quote from Kingery's diary letters:

"We was [sic] informed that the citizens of Shasta had prepared a dinner at the St. Charles Hotel for the emegrants [sic]...We was [sic] the first train of waggons [sic] that ever come [sic] into Shasta on the Shasta or Knobles Rout [sic]." - Solomon Kingery, Aug 22, 1852
——Marker is in Shasta, California, in Shasta County. Marker is at the intersection of 15432 Eureka Way (California Route 299) and 2nd Street, on the right when traveling west on 15432 Eureka Way.

"Traveld 7 miles. Road very hard to brake on account of stone & chaperal brush. Encamped on Rassberry (Manzanita) Creek. Grass rather (poor) but abundenc(e) of Mt Rassberrys." - Solomon Kingery, Aug 17, 1852
——Marker is near Summertown, California, in Shasta County. Marker is on Forest Route 17, 0.1 miles south of California Route 44, on the left when traveling south.

Kingery mentions I. Grush in his journal:
...(April) 9th. Bill 62 1/2 for hay. Corn could not be got here. Traveld 17 miles to Dalberts, 1 miles west of Snookes grove, Potowa Co. The Co. Seat is 10 miles south of this. Here the Citizence had a Spelling School, Wm. Sadler, I. Grush, T. Biggins & my Self speld with them.
["I" is probably a typo..."J"?]

There was often trouble with Native Americans along the way as the Indians would rustle the Waggoners' cattle. One incident is documented by Kingery and in the diary of Adam Baker Carlock which appears in *History of the Carlock Family* by Marion Pomeroy Carlock. (see Appendix I comparing the two diaries). Carlock's company traveled along with Kingery's for part of the trip.

Kingery mentions John and James Grush in a letter to his parents, Shasta City, April 12th, 1853:
... Daniel & Harris are well & are mining on Trinity R., yet, and are Making a living. James Grush, and Wm. Sadler are are at the Same place & are well. I met John Grush to day Going over on the Trinity from here. He is well and he showed me a letter Which he had Just Recd from his father Which I was glad to See, & he also Informed mc that he got one from his sister Mary.
(see Appendix J, transcript of letter)

More about Solomon Kingery:
Born in Dauphin Co. Pa in 1831. Died while in California on 1831 Jul-9-1855, aged 24 yrs, 3 mo. He is buried in the Shasta Union Cemetery In the town of Shasta, 3 miles west of Redding.

In 2013 I published my second novel, again based on family history, *Once Upon a Gold Rush*, ISBN-13: 978-0-615-90024-7 (Broadhorn Publishing). It chronicled John and James on their journey to California, closely following Kingery's journal. I added sister Mary and her future husband, Charles Ayres to the California narratives, although they were not there…poetic license. A third section of my novel dealt with the mystery of what happened to James. I fantasized that he wandered off, was attacked by a bear on Mount Shasta, married a Native American girl and had a child, then became a hermit living high on the mountain. At the time of the writing I had no knowledge of James' history after the mention of him at Trinity in1853. More on this later. In my research I came upon two unsubstantiated rumors about John. I heard from someone that "one of the brothers traveled around the Horn and survived a shipwreck." And a story related by a relative suggested that Joaquin Miller may have written about John Grush in one of his books, but I wasn't able to find any mention of him in Miller's writings.

More about John Grush:
From the Ogle County Press, Saturday, January 2nd, 1886:
…John Grush recently sold to George Traver a few acres of land near Rock River. Including the famous "Steeple Rook" which, If the C. B, & N. R. R. Co. establishes a Summer Resort along Rock River, will perhaps make "Yorob von rich mans," as the towering bluff is one of the most important points of interest and scenery for the pleasure seeker. This place Is familiar to Pine Creekers as the accustomed grounds for picnics.
[I have been unable to identify what and where Steeple Rock may be. However, John's farm in Pine Creek Township was very close to the Rock River and the town of Oregon, Illinois, where another "towering bluff" is located, called Castle Rock, in what is now Castle Rock State Park. And this from the Ogle County Historical Society: "In the 1890s the RR did establish what they advertised as a summer resort but it was the Oregon area on the Eagle's Nest Bluff popularized by Margaret Fuller when she came to this area in 1843 and wrote "Ganymede To His Eagle" in which she mentions the spring (later named Ganymede spring in her honor) and the eagle's nest tree and bluff on which Lorado Taft would build his Eternal Indian, commonly referred to as the Black Hawk statue." Interesting.]

Children of JOHN GRUSH and MARY TENNIS are:

  i. IDA MAY[6] GRUSH, b. June 22, 1861, Ogle Co., IL; d. September 18, 1947, Albion, Marshall Co., IA; m. LYMAN CHASE PRICE, February 10, 1886, Ogle Co., IL; b. December 19, 1856, Pine Creek Twp., Ogle Co., IL (living in IA in 1899); d. July 26, 1925, Albion, Marshall Co., IA.

  More About IDA MAY GRUSH:
  Burial: Bethel Grove Cemetery, Albion, Marshall Co., IA

  More About LYMAN CHASE PRICE:
  Burial: Bethel Grove Cemetery, Albion, Marshall Co., IA

  More about Lyman Chase PRICE and Ida May GRUSH :
  Lyman Chase PRICE (John W PRICE6, John PRICE5, Jacob PRICE4, John PRICE3, Johannes PREISS2, Johan Jakob PREISS1) was born 19 DEC 1856 in Pine Creek Township, Ogle, Illinois, and died 26 JUL 1925. He married Ida May GRUSH 10 FEB 1886, daughter of John GRUSH and Mary Jane. She was born 22 JUN 1861.
  Children of Lyman Chase PRICE and Ida May GRUSH are:
    i.   Bessie Pearl PRICE was born 6 JAN 1887, and died 10 MAR 1903.
    ii.   Mary Jane PRICE was born 5 OCT 1888 in Huron, Beadle, South Dakota. She married Adrian SWEELY 10 FEB 1921, son of Henry SWEELY and Louisa HUP.

More About MARY JANE PRICE:
Residence: Rodman, Palo Alto Co., IA (last known)

More About ADRIAN SWEELY:
Occupation: Postmaster, merchant, Rodman, Iowa

    iii.   Mabel PRICE was born 13 NOV 1890 in State Center, Marshall, Iowa.
    iv.   Edith PRICE was born 30 SEP 1892.
    v.   Ada PRICE was born 18 SEP 1894. She married Edwin Clyde PORTER.
    vi.   John W PRICE was born 12 AUG 1898.
    vii.   Charles W PRICE was born 2 OCT 1902.
    viii.   Lester T PRICE was born 9 APR 1906.

Mrs. Ida Price, 84, Is Dead at Albion
Albion — (Special) — Mrs. Ida May Price B4, resident of Albion for 47 years, died at 7:4S a. m Thursday. following an extended illness of the infirmities of old age. She was born Ida May Grush, June 21, 1863 in Ogle county, 111. On Feb. 19, 1886 she married L. C. Price at Pine Creek, III. And they moved to Wolsey, S. D. where they lived for several years. In 1900 they moved to a farm two miles northeast of Albion where they lived until 1924 when they moved to a house they had purchased in Albion. Mr.Price died July 3d, 1925. Mrs. Price is survived by six children, six grandchildren and three great grandchildren. The children are: Mrs. A. P. Sweely, Rodman; Mrs. J. N. McKibbeh, Garwin Wilbur, Emmetsburg; Mrs. E. C. Porter, Marshalltown; John Price and Mrs. Harry Wilkerson, both ot Albion; Funeral services Will be con-ducted Saturday at 10:30 a. m. at the Bethel Grove church with Rev. George Blersborn and ReV. P. K Peterson in charge. Burial will be In the Bethel Grove cemetery. The body it at the Pursel funeral home in Marshalltown.

  ii. HATTIE EMMA[6] GRUSH, b. March 05, 1866, Polo, Buffalo Twp., Ogle Co., IL; d. October 09 1943, Belvidere, Boone Co., IL.

More about HATTIE EMMA GRUSH:
She married WILLIAM EDMUND HORNER December 10, 1885, in Polo, Buffalo Twp., Ogle Co., IL, son of PETER HORNER and WILHELMINA BIESECKER. He was born May 30, 1861 in Lanark, Carroll Co., IL (appears in 1910 and 1930 Rock Creek Twp., Carroll Co., IL census), and died January 10, 1940 in Lanark, Carroll Co., IL.

More About HATTIE EMMA GRUSH:
Burial: Lanark Cemetery, Lanark, Rock Creek Twp., Carroll Co., IL

More About WILLIAM EDMUND HORNER:
Burial: Lanark Cemetery, Lanark, Rock Creek Twp., Carroll Co., IL

Children of HATTIE GRUSH and WILLIAM HORNER are:
    i.   CLAUDE ALBERT[7] HORNER, b. February 1887, IL (appears in 1910 Rock Creek Twp., Carroll Co., IL census); d. January 20, 1945, Rockford, Winnebago Co., IL; m. BESSIE L. CROUSE; b. March 1887, WI; d. September 05, 1929, Rockford, Winnebago Co., IL.
    ii.   RALPH RAYMOND HORNER, b. March 22, 1893, Lanark, Carroll Co., IL (appears in 1930 Lima Twp., Carroll Co., IL census); d. February 17, 1973, Seattle, King Co., WA.

  iii. ALEXANDER JAMES[6] GRUSH, b. July 14, 1869, Ogle Co., IL (appears in 1900 Pine Creek Twp., Ogle Co., IL census); d. April 01, 1945, Aurora, Kane Co., IL., July 12, 2013

More about ALEXANDER JAMES[6] GRUSH:
He married IDA BIRDELLEN TOMS November 09, 1893 in Ogle Co., IL, daughter of CHARLES TOMS and MARY WOLTZ. She was born March 01, 1874 in Ogle Co., IL, and died May 05, 1965 in Aurora, Kane Co., IL.

From Alexander Grush obituary:
Death Claims Former Naperville Mayor

Alexander J. Grush, former mayor of Naperville died at Copley Hospital, Aurora on Sunday April 1, 1945. Following the funeral services at the Methodist church on Thursday afternoon April 5th, Masonic burial rites were conducted at the Naperville cemetery
Mr. Grush had been active for many years in civil affairs, serving as commissioner from 1917 until 1921, when he was selected to fill the unexpired term of Mayor Charles Bowman [in Naperville, IL]. He served as mayor for two years. He was elected to the same office in 1931 for a regular four-year term.
Born in Ogle County, Illinois, on July 14, 1869, Mr. Grush was in the meat business in Polo and Sycamore before coming to Naperville in 1907. While here he established the Grush Oil Company at 309 N. Washington St. Surviving him are his wife, Mrs. Ida B. Grush, three children, Vernon C. Grush of Downers Grove, Mrs. Homer Boelter of California, and Byron E. Grush of Naperville, a sister, Mrs. Ray Price of Albion, Iowa, and seven grandchildren. Mr. Grush was a member of Euclid Lodge No. 65, A.F.& A.M., members of which conducted the service at the cemetery. Rev. Wesley M. Westerberg was the officiating minister at the church and Marjorie Stauss was the organist. [Submitted by Byron Grush, transcribed by Kris Dunlap]

More about Alex Grush under Generation 6.

Child of JOHN GRUSH and ANNIE LEE is:

OTIS JOHN[6] GRUSH, b. August 18, 1872, Ogle Co., IL; d. May 24, 1899. He married (2) MARY VIOLA BAIN December 07, 1893 in Oregon, Ogle Co., IL, daughter of SANDERS BAIN and NANCY LOOKABAUGH. She was born February 29, 1872 in Clarion Co., PA (appears in 1900, 1910 and 1920 Mt. Morris, Mt. Morris Twp., Ogle Co., IL census), and died December 26, 1961.

More About OTIS JOHN GRUSH:
Burial: Fairmount Cemetery, Polo, Buffalo Twp., Ogle Co., IL

More About MARY VIOLA BAIN:
Burial: Fairmount Cemetery, Polo, Buffalo Twp., Ogle Co., IL

Children of OTIS GRUSH and MARY BAIN are:
ii. GERTRUDE ANN[7] GRUSH, b. December 18, 1894, IL (appears in 1920 Mt. Morris, Mt. Morris Twp., Ogle Co., IL census); d. 1957.

More About GERTRUDE ANN GRUSH:
Burial: Fairmount Cemetery, Polo, Buffalo Twp., Ogle Co., IL

iii. GLADYS MILDRED GRUSH, b. July 01, 1896, IL; d. August 01, 1988, Mt. Morris, Ogle Co., IL.
iv. BOYD J. GRUSH, b. September 10, 1897, IL (appears in 1920 Mt. Morris, Mt. Morris Twp., Ogle Co., IL census); d. June 16, 1948, Mt. Morris, Ogle Co., IL.

More About BOYD J. GRUSH:
Burial: Fairmount Cemetery, Polo, Buffalo Twp., Ogle Co., IL

Military service: WW I. Injured with shrapnel in legs. Nickname, "Peck."
Wife, Lillian Elizabeth Judge was born in Cleveland, Ohio on July 10, 1898. Her parents were Patrick Judge and Catherine Costella.

Obit:
Boyd J. Grush Mt. Morris, 1ll., June 16.—Boyd J. Grush, 50, died of a heart ailment -this morning at 4:30 in his home. He had been ill for the past ten years and bedfast for the past month. He was born in Mt. Morris township Sept. 10, 1897, the son of Mary (Bain) and Otis Grush. He was a veteran of World War I. Surviving is his wife, Lillian Grush, a daughter, Mary Kathryn and his mother. Three sisters, Miss Maude C., Miss Gertrude Ann, and Mrs. Gladys M. Jones also survive. Funeral services will be held Friday at the home at 1:30 and at 2 p. m, at-Trinity Lutheran church, Rev. Alfred Stone will officiate and burial will be in Fairmount cemetery at Polo.
———June 16, 1948, Freeport Journal-Standard from Freeport, Illinois · Page 11

  5. WILLIAM[5] GRUSH (ISAAC[4], PHILIP[3], CHRISTOPHER[2], JOSEPH[1]) was born November 20, 1829 in Huntingdon Co., PA (appears in 1860 Pine Creek Twp., Ogle Co., IL census), and died May 06, 1902 in Dresden, Chickasaw Co., IA. He married CATHERINE TENNIS (sister of Mary Jane Tennis who married JOHN[5] GRUSH) November 07, 1852 in Ogle Co., IL. She was born Abt. 1832 in IN., died December 30, 1871. He married Emma Clammer, of Mahaska County, September 19, 1872.

Children of WILLIAM GRUSH and CATHERINE TENNIS are:
    i.   JOHN[6] J. GRUSH, b. March 23, 1855, IL.
    ii. FRANCES M. GRUSH, b. November 1, . 1857, IL.
    iii. Chas. H. GRUSH b. April 12, 1860; died July 26, 1875
    iv   Cora D. GRUSH, b. November 15, 1865
         More about Cora Delyle Reasoner:
         Married Willis Augustus Reasoner Feb 9 1886
         Death Elgin, Fayette, Iowa, USA, 1902
    v.   William I. GRUSH, b. November 25, 1868, died 1942

Children of WILLIAM GRUSH and EMMA CLAMMER are:
    i.   Mary L. GRUSH, b. August 23, 1873
    ii. Lotta M. GRUSH b. July 22, 1875; died January 26, 1879
    iii. David R. b. May 19, 1878

More about William Grush:
GRUSH, WILLIAM—Deep River Twp. Druggist, Dresden, P.O. Deep River. Was born in Huntingdon County, Pennsylvania, November 20, 1829, and worked on his father's farm until he was twenty-one years old, when he apprenticed himself to learn the trade of shoemaking, at which he worked one year. He then went to Buffalo, Illinois, where he found employment for one year. After this he was employed by the Illinois Central Railroad. After a short time he established himself at his trade in Eagle Point, Illinois, where he remained about six years, when, his health being impaired, he sold out and rented a farm, upon which he remained till April 21, 1867. He then came to Iowa, and purchased a farm of eighty acres near Dresden. After farming a few years he bought property in Dresden and again resumed his trade, until May 1, 1877, when he bought his present business. Mr. Grush has been twice married, his first wife being Miss Catharine Tennes, [Tennis] of Buffalo, Illinois, who bore him the following children: John J. (born March 23, 1855), Francis M. (born November 1, 1857), Chas. H. (born April 12, 1860; died July 26, 1875), Effie A. (born March 14, 1863), Cora D. (born November 15, 1865) and William I. (born November 25, 1868). His first wife died December 30, 1871, and for his second wife he married Emma Clammer, of Mahaska county, September 19, 1872. The children by this marriage are as follows: Mary L. (born August 23, 1873), Lotta M. (born July 22, 1875; died January 26, 1879) and David R. (born May 19, 1878). Mr. Grush has served his township as constable for seven consecutive years.
———http://www.rootsweb.ancestry.com/~iabiog/poweshiek/hp1880/deepriver-dh.htm

William Grush 1829 - 1902

More about John James GRUSH, 1855-1923:
John James GRUSH was born on month day 1855, at birthplace, Illinois, to WILLIAM GRUSH and Catherine GRUSH (born TENNIS). WILLIAM was born on November 20 1829, in Shirleysburg, Huntington, PA. Catherine was born on October 2 1832, in Allen, IN. John had 10 siblings: Francis Marion GRUSH, Charles Henry GRUSH and 8 other siblings. John married Mary Etta GRUSH (born FOULK) on month day 1878, at age 23 at marriage place, Illinois. Mary was born on January 21 1860, in Davis, Iowa. They had 2 sons: William A. GRUSH and one other child. John passed away on month day 1923, at age 68 at death place, Montana. He was buried at burial place, Montana.
——http://www.myheritage.com/names/john_grush

William Isaac Grush 1869 - 1942

5.   JAMES[5] GRUSH (ISAAC[4], PHILIP[3], CHRISTOPHER[2], JOSEPH[1]) was born in Shirleysburg, Huntingdon Co., PA. to Isaac and Catharine (Burns) Grush, and moved with the family to Pine Creek, Illinois in 1846. Died possibly 1860 in California.

More about James Grush:
From A BRIEF HISTORY OF THE GRUSH FAMILY, W. E. Bomberger, Gowrie, Iowa:
…As to the family history of his children I believe that each have children or grandchildren who can do better than I. Except possibly Uncle Jim. Mother told me that he and Uncle John went to California in the mad gold rush, in 1852, and that after great hardships they got through. Then the brothers got separated and to my knowledge none of his family have ever heard anything from him since. Uncle John had to return without him. In after years much time and money were spent in trying to locate him, but without any results.

From Ken Ryan family tree, descendant of William, brother of John and James:
James Grush b. Abt. 1832, Huntingdon Co., PA. Death: 1860 in California, FAMILY HISTORY COMPILED BY BERYL WEGENER; JOHN GRUSH AND JAMES WENT TO CALIFORNIA TO WORK THE GOLDMINES, JOHN CAME BACK ALONE AND JAMES WAS NEVER HEARD FROM AGAIN.

From Van Kirk, Susie, "Fort Humboldt Conflict Period" [items from the Humboldt Times]:

(Humboldt Times Editor Edwin D. Coleman 9 Sept. 1854 to 5 Jan. 1856.)
HT (23 Sept. 1854) Indian Murder—On Monday morning, the 18th inst., Mr. Arthur Wigmore of St. Louis, Missouri, an Irishman by birth, was killed at the lower Rancheree on Weeott river about a half a mile from his house. (see Appendix K for details of this and other incidents)

HT (30 Sept. 1854) We with pleasure give place to the following contradiction of the statement we published in our last number. Our information was obtained from Mr. Robinson....Eel River, Sept. 27, 1854. Editor of Humboldt Times: We, the company that went in search of the murderers of Wigmore, a few days ago, take this opportunity of informing you that you were misinformed, either malignantly of through ignorance concerning the conduct of said company and particularly as to the committal of violence upon the person of a squaw, by one of our party. G.A. and Thomas Dungan, A. Denman, G.W. Larimore, J.F. Whiten, W. Minor, J. Ripley, James Grush, W.H. Gilman, J.S. Ball.

(Humboldt Editor Austin Wiley, 23 Jan. 1858 to 16 June 1860)
HT (19 June 1858) Don't Like It—Some men in the lower end of the county are very indignant at our article last week, concerning the Indian difficulty on Eel river and the character of the men who did the shooting. They think we did wrong in giving the names of some of the parties. All we regret is that we did not have all their names, so we could hold them up to the public as they deserve. Two men named Wideman and Grush, we have since learned, were leaders in this cowardly attack. They are said to be bad men and continually creating trouble with the Indians....

p.s. Since the above was in type, we learn that Sherman has been surrendered by his bondsman to the Sheriff and is now in jail, awaiting the action of the Grand Jury

HT (26 June 1858) Grand Jury Report—indictments against Sherman, McDonald, Baker, Wideman and Grush for murder.

[There were no further reports on the results of this indictment from the paper. Often men arrested for the murder of Indians were acquitted in those days. Interesting enough, the editors of the Humboldt Times advocated vigilant action against the indigenous peoples of the area: "Our mode of warfare with Indians is to pay them off in their own coin. If they murder a white man without cause, kill then Indians for it." In fact, one of the most horrendous genocides in California history took place there two years later: "The 1860 Wiyot Massacre took place on Indian Island in the spring of 1860, committed by a group of locals thought to be composed primarily of Eureka businessmen. (The male Wiyot tribal members had left the island during their annual New Year ritual and the vigilantes killed as many as 250 children, women, and elderly tribal members)" ——https://en.wikipedia.org/wiki/Eureka,_California. The vigilantes were called the Eel River Raiders.]

5. MARY JANE[5] GRUSH (ISAAC[4], PHILIP[3], CHRISTOPHER[2], JOSEPH[1]) was born March 07, 1834 in Huntingdon Co., PA (appears in 1900 and 1910 Woosung Twp., Ogle Co., IL census), and died April 27, 1924 in Woosung Twp., Ogle Co., IL. She married CHARLES H. AYRES June 01, 1854 [1855?] in Stephenson Co., IL, son of LUDLAM AYRES and SUSANNA SHARER. He was born September 13, 1824 in Huntingdon Co., PA (appears in 1860, 1870 and 1880 Buffalo Twp., Ogle Co., IL census), and died November 01, 1880 in Woosung Twp., Ogle Co., IL.

More About MARY JANE GRUSH:
Burial: Palmyra Cemetery, Palmyra Twp., Lee Co., IL

More About CHARLES HENRY AYRES:
Burial: Palmyra Cemetery, Palmyra Twp., Lee Co., IL

Obit:
Mary Jane Grush was born in Lancaster Co. Penn., March 7. 1831.She died In Woosung township, in the home in which she had lived for the past 66 years, on last Sunday evening. April 27. at 7:15 Her age was 90 years, I month, and 20 days. When she was 12 years old she came with her parents, Isaac and Catherine Grush and other members of the family from the Pennsylvania home, overland by wagon to the Ohio river, and down the Ohio to the Mississippi and up the Mississippi by boat, then by wagon again across the country, settling in Pine Creek township. Her mother's father was a soldier in the Revolution.

Her mother's father was a soldier of the Revolution. She continued to live with her parents in the Pine Creek home until June 1, I855. when she was married to Charles H. Ayres. They went to housekeeping In the township in which they were married, and about two years later moved to Woosung Township, settling on the farm that has been her home ever since. Here, having scoured material for their new home, they had the disappointing experience of having it all destroyed by a prairie fire before the house was constructed. They then bought a small building near where Dixon now stands and by ox team hauled it to the farm and it became their new home.

To Mr and Mrs. Ayres were born eight children, four sons and four daughters. John E., Charles and Lena May died In Infancy. Elsie M died at the age of 26. and Henry P when 26. The father and husbandwent to his eternal reward November 1, 1880. The children who survive are Samuel R. of Falls City. Nebraska, Alma S. Parks, of the homestead. and Lillie S. Lampln of Polo. Together with these there remain two sisters, Mrs. Emma Arnold of Freeport and Mrs. Catherine Palmatier of Thornburg, Iowa, and one brother, David R. Grush of Falls City. Nebraska. These sisters were unable to be present because of ill health. Mother Ayres had just two grandchildren.

Mrs. Ayres became a Christian in youth and has been a devout and godly woman through a long and active life. She early Identified herself with the church and for more than thirty years has been an attendant and member of the East Jordan church. She knew the happy secret of that trust in God that kept her life serene and beautiful in the home, in the church, anal among all who knew her. In pioneer days, when people were tested in unusual ways, these elements in her character meant much and proved of great worth. There was a cheerfulness and brightness about her that always drew people to her. Children and young people loved her dearly. The passing of such a life leaves behind a blessing and a benediction.

The funeral was held Wednesday afternoon. April 30, at the home in Woosung Township at two o'clock and at 2:30 at the Sugar Grove church. Rev. M. B. Leach had charge of the services. At the home Mrs. Reed and Mrs. Ballou. of Dixon sang "Lead Kindly Light." and Rev B. Lee Towsley offered prayer in the church. Rev. Isaac Summers of Ridott read the 21st Psalm, and Rev Leach led in prayer. Mr. Towsley of Adair preached the sermon from John 14 1 and Mr. Leach read the obituary and delivered a short address. Mrs. Reed and Mrs Ballou sang "At Evening Time It shall Be Light," "Home of the Soul," and "Abide With Me." Burial was made in Sugar Grove cemetery.
——From Tri-County Press, Polo, Illinois, Thursday, May 8th, 1924

Children of MARY GRUSH and CHARLES AYRES are:
     I   ELSIE MARY[6] AYRES, b. June 17, 1856, IL; d. June 02, 1892.
         More About ELSIE MAY AYRES:
         Burial: Palmyra Cemetery, Palmyra Twp., Lee Co., IL

    ii   SAMUEL R. AYRES, b. December 28, 1857, IL (living in Hardin Co., IA in 1899).
    iii   JOHNNIE E. AYRES, b. December 28, 1859, IL; d. January 15, 1861.

More About JOHNNIE E. AYRES:
Burial: Palmyra Cemetery, Palmyra Twp., Lee Co., IL

iv ALMA SUSAN AYRES, b. January 15, 1861, IL. (appears in 1940 Woosung Twp., Ogle Co., IL census); d. February 23, 1955, Polo, Buffalo Twp., Ogle Co., IL.

v LILLIE SARAH AYRES, b. December 31, 1863, IL; d. August 27, 1947, Sterling, Whiteside Co., IL; m. JOHN C. LAMPIN, December 12, 1883, Ogle Co., IL; b. November 1862, IL (appears in 1900 Mt. Morris, Mt. Morris Twp., 1910, 1920 and 1930 Polo, Buffalo Twp., Ogle Co., IL census); d. 1949.

More About LILLIE SARAH AYRES:
Burial: Fairmount Cemetery, Polo, Buffalo Twp., Ogle Co., IL

More About JOHN C. LAMPIN:
Burial: Fairmount Cemetery, Polo, Buffalo Twp., Ogle Co., IL

vi CHARLES AYRES, b. August 05, 1866, IL; d. March 17, 1867.
vii HENRY P. AYRES, b. August 15, 1869, IL; d. June 06, 1895.
viii LENA MAY AYRES, b. June 28, 1872; d. February 06, 1875.
More About LENA MAY AYRES:
Burial: Palmyra Cemetery, Palmyra Twp., Lee Co., IL

More about Charles Ayres:
CHARLES AYRES, deceased, was a prominent farmer of Woosung township, one well known in Lee and Ogle counties. He was born in Huntingdon county, Pennsylvania, September 13, 1824, and was the son of Ludlum and Susanna (Sharer) Ayres, who emigrated from Pennsylvania to Illinois in 1845, locating in Franklin Grove, Lee county, where they remained until 1860, when they moved to the southern part of the state, where they spent about one year, and then returned to Lee county, where the remainder of their lives were spent. They had a family of eight children, two of whom died in childhood. Those growing to maturity were Charles H., Matthew, John, William, Thomas and Ludlum Smith.

The subject of this sketch spent his boyhood and youth in his native state, and in the schools of that state received his education. This was, however, supplemented by attendance in the schools of Dixon, after the removal of the family to this state. He remained with his parents until twenty-two years old, when he began life for himself, cultivating a farm and operating two threshing machines during the seasons. He was united in marriage June I, 1855, with Miss Mary J. Grush, who was born March 7, 1834, and daughter of Isaac and Catherine (Burns) Grush, the former a native of Lancaster County, Pennsylvania, and the latter of Huntingdon County, in the same state. Isaac Grush was the son of Isaac Grush, Sr., a native of Germany, and a farmer by occupation, who died in Lancaster County, Pennsylvania. Isaac Grush was by trade a miller, and also followed the trade of cooper. In 1846 he came with his family to Ogle county, and located in Pine Creek township, where he purchased a farm of one hundred and sixty acres, which he operated until within a few years before his death, when he retired from active life, and died at the residence of his son in Paul City, Nebraska.

Isaac and Catherine Grush were the parents of ten children, eight of whom grew to maturity—Philip, John, William, James, Mary J., Elizabeth, Emma and Catherine. Two died in infancy. Mrs. Catherine Grush passed to her reward in 1851, and later Mr. Grush married Mrs. Catherine (Lutz) Eshelman, a widow, and by this marriage there was one daughter, Vernie.

To Charles and Mary J. Ayres eight children were born. Elsie M., born June 17, 1856, died June 2, 1892. Samuel R., born December 28, 1857, is now living in Hardin county, Iowa; he married Miss Delia Miller, of

Washington county, Maryland, and they have a son, Charles L. Johnnie E., born December 28, 1859, died January 15, 1861. Alma S., born January 15, r86i, is now the wife of C. E. Parks, and they have one child, Clarence C., born January i, 1888; they reside on the old homestead. Lillie S., born December 31, 1863, married John Lampin, and they live in Pine Creek township. Henry P., born August 15, 1869, died June 6, 1895. Charles, born August 5, 1866, died March 17, 1867. Lena May, born June 28, 1872, died Feb. 6, 1875.

Mr. Ayres purchased the farm on which his widow now resides, on section 8, Woosung township, from his brother William, who entered the land from the government. In 1855, soon after his marriage, he built a small house, which is now used as an ice house. The second house in which the family lived was erected a few years after, and is now used as a shop. In 1874 he erected the house in which the family now live, and which is a commodious and comfortable structure. As his means would permit, Mr. Ayers added to the improvements of the place, erecting a large barn, and putting up other outbuildings, setting out fruit and ornamental trees, and otherwise adding to the attractive appearance of the farm. He was a practical farmer and endeavored to keep up with the times in the way of improvements.

In politics, Mr. Ayres was a Republican, and a stanch advocate of the principles of the party. He served his neighborhood as school director for a number of years, as he always felt an interest in the public schools. He was also road commissioner a number of years. Religiously he was a member of the United Brethren church, in which he took great interest, being a firm believer in the Christian religion. His wife is also a member of that church. Mr. Ayres passed from this life November I, 1880, his death being from asthma and consumption. He was a good man, and his death was a sad loss not only to his faithful wife, who was always a comfort and stay to him, but to the community as well. His friends were numerous in both Lee and Ogle counties.

——The Biographical record of Ogle County, Illinois By S.J. Clarke Publishing Company, 1899, p. 76.

5. ELIZABETH[5] GRUSH (ISAAC[4], PHILIP[3], CHRISTOPHER[2], JOSEPH[1]) was born May 03, 1836 in Huntingdon Co., PA, and died February 07, 1913 in Gowrie, Webster Co., IA. She married JOSIAH SNYDER BOMBERGER October 14, 1858 in Ogle Co., IL, son of JOHN BOMBERGER and MARY SNYDER. He was born August 16, 1837 in Washington Co., MD (appears in 1860 and 1870 Buffalo Twp., Ogle Co., IL census), and died January 31, 1913 in Gowrie, Webster Co., IA.

More About ELIZABETH GRUSH:
Burial: Gowrie Cemetery, Gowrie, Webster Co., IA

More About JOSIAH SNYDER BOMBERGER:
Burial: Gowrie Cemetery, Gowrie, Webster Co., IA

Elizabeth (Grush) Bomberger 1836-1913, obituary

Elizabeth Grush was born at Huntingdon County, Penn., on 3 May 1836, and died at her home in Gowrie, on 7 Feb 1913, at the age of 76 years, 9 months and 4 days.

When she was 11 years of age she came west with her father's family. They came first on a flat boat down the Conemaugh, Alleghany and Ohio rivers to the junction with the Mississippi and were towed by behind a steamboat to Savannah, Ill. Here they were met by friends who had preceded them. They then went to the place that is now known as Polo, Ill.

One of the deceased's vivid recollections of the trip, was that of seeing the Mormons fleeing from Nauvo, Ill., across the Mississippi to commence their long journey to Utah. The hardships and privations which she with the rest of the family endured in those pioneer days were indeed many.

On 14 Oct 1858 she was united in marriage to Josiah S. Bomberger, who passed to his reward just 7 days previous to her demise. They had lived happily together for nearly 55 years. To this union five children were born, all of whom survive. They are:
1. W. E. Bomberger of Gowrie [William Edward]
2. Mrs. R. C. Smythe of Marreta, Minn [Mary Ellen]
3. Mrs G. E. Briggs of Wilmont, Minn [Ida W.]
4. M. H. Bomberger of Parks, Neb [Marcus Herman]
5. Mrs F. E. Wells of Grinnell, Iowa [Irena May]

Besides the children she is survived by three sisters and one brother:
Mrs John Arnold of Freeport, Ill
Mrs Charles Ayers of Polo, Ill
Mrs Jessee Palmeten of Thornburg, Iowa
Mr David Grush of Falls City, Neb

In 1856 she with her husband joined the United Brethren church and remained with that church for 5 years after which they both united with the Christian church and remained in that faith until death. Mrs. Bomberger was a faithful Christian wife and mother and was always wanting to help others, but never willing for anyone to wait on her.

Her sudden death is a great shock to her children and friends, who deeply mourn her demise. She was willing and anxious to go and we comfort ourselves with the thought that our loss is her gain. She is united so soon with her husband in Heaven. The funeral services were held at the Congregational church here on last Sunday afternoon, conducted by Rev D. G. Youker. Interment was made in the Gowrie cemetery.

Children of ELIZABETH GRUSH and JOSIAH BOMBERGER are:
    i.   WILLIAM EDWARD[6] BOMBERGER, b. July 19, 1859, Polo, Buffalo Twp., Ogle Co., IL; d. August 29, 1937, Gowrie, Webster Co., IA; m. INEZ GERTRUDE SORBER, December 22, 1886.

        More About WILLIAM EDWARD BOMBERGER:
        Burial: Gowrie Cemetery, Gowrie, Webster Co., IA

        More About INEZ GERTRUDE SORBER:
        Burial: Gowrie Twp. Cemetery, Gowrie, Webster Co., I

    ii.   MARY ELLEN BOMBERGER, b. June 17, 1862, Polo, Buffalo Twp., Ogle Co., IL; d. September 10, 1943, Gowrie, Webster Co., IA; m. ROBERT COLWELL SMYTHE, December 23, 1882; b. March 20, 1854, OH; d. May 14, 1941.More About MARY ELLEN BOMBERGER:
        Burial: Gowrie Twp. Cemetery, Gowrie, Webster Co., IA

        More About ROBERT COLWELL SMYTHE:
        Burial: Gowrie Twp. Cemetery, Gowrie, Webster Co., IA

    iii.   IDA WINONA BOMBERGER, b. August 03, 1863, Polo, Buffalo Twp., Ogle Co., IL; d. January 21, 1930, Humboldt, Humboldt Co., IA; m. GEORGE EDGAR BRIGGS, March 30, 1884; b. December 09, 1860; d. September 19, 1948.

        More About IDA WINONA BOMBERGER:
        Burial: Gowrie Twp. Cemetery, Gowrie, Webster Co., IA

        More About GEORGE EDGAR BRIGGS:
        Burial: Gowrie Twp. Cemetery, Gowrie, Webster Co., IA

iv. MARCUS HERMAN BOMBERGER, b. March 10, 1872, Polo, Buffalo Twp., Ogle Co., IL; d. August 18, 1936, McCook, Red Willow Co., NE; m. OLIVE DOWD, April 23, 1907; b. March 12, 1883; d. July 12, 1936, Hastings, Adams Co., NE.

More About MARCUS HERMAN BOMBERGER:
Burial: Benkelman Cemetery, Benkelman, Dundy Co., NE

More About OLIVE DOWD:
Burial: Benkelman Cemetery, Benkelman, Dundy Co., NE

v. IRENA MAE BOMBERGER, b. January 09, 1874, Polo, Buffalo Twp., Ogle Co., IL; d. October 04, 1914, Grinnell, Poweshiek Co., IA; m. FRED ELDRIDGE WELLS, December 21, 1892, Gowrie, Webster Co., IA; b. December 22, 1863, NY; d. 1934.

More About IRENA MAE BOMBERGER:
Burial: Gowrie Twp. Cemetery, Gowrie, Webster Co., IA

More About FRED ELDRIDGE WELLS:
Burial: Hazelwood Cemetery, Grinnell, Poweshiek Co., IA

5. EMMA[5] GRUSH (ISAAC[4], PHILIP[3], CHRISTOPHER[2], JOSEPH[1]) was born June 17, 1840 in Huntingdon Co., PA, and died April 03, 1929 in Freeport, Stephenson Co., IL. She married JOHN DAVID ARNOLD March 21, 1861 in Ogle Co., IL, son of DANIEL ARNOLD and CATHARINE ?. He was born May 12, 1839 in OH (appears in 1870 Haldane Twp. and 1880 Haldane Village, Lincoln Twp., Ogle Co., IL census), and died January 02, 1919.

Notes for EMMA GRUSH:
Emma Grush ARNOLD
Mrs. Emma Grush Arnold, widow of John D. Arnold, passed away April 3, 1929 at 11:15 A. M. at the home of her son, Dr. B. A. Arnold, 320 North Galena Avenue, Freeport. Her death was caused by old age. Interment was in Fairmount Cemetery. Emma Grush Arnold was born in Lancaster County, near Lancaster Pa., June 17, 1840. Had she lived two and one-half months longer she would have reached the age of 89 years. She was the daughter of Isaac and Catherine Grush. In the spring of 1845 she moved with her family westward. They traveled by team and boat on the Ohio river and along the Mississippi to Savanna, Ill., and settled in Ogle County, in Pine Creek Township. Here Emma Grush grew to womanhood. In 1860 she became the wife of John D. Arnold, deceased Jan 2nd, 1919. The young couple made their home near Mount Morris, Ill. Of this union four children were born: Dr. B. A. Arnold, A. J. Arnold of Freeport, Ill., Dr. W. D. Arnold of Spokane, Wash., and one daughter who passed away in infancy. One sister also survives, Mrs. Catherine Palmatier, Thornberg, Ia., and a half sister, Mrs. Vernie Johnson, Meeker, Okla., and two step sisters, Mrs. N. D. Hersch, Waterloo, Ia., and Mrs. Elsie Reed, Kansas City, Mo. Many nieces and nephews of the deceased are also surviving. For 33 years this family lived in Ogle County. In 1893 they moved to Chicago. In 1895 they and their three sons located in Freeport. For the last few years Mrs. Arnold made her home with Sr. and Mrs. B. A. Arnold at 320 N. Galena Avenue. She was a faithful member of Second Presbyterian Church and was a woman of sterling worth, a kind neighbor and faithful friend. In pioneer days when doctors and nurses were few she gave unselfish service in her community. Until about ten days before her passing on, Mrs. Arnold enjoyed excellent health and was unusually active for a woman of her age.

More About EMMA GRUSH:
Burial: Fairmount Cemetery, Polo, Buffalo Twp., Ogle Co., IL

More About JOHN DAVID ARNOLD:
Burial: Fairmount Cemetery, Polo, Buffalo Twp., Ogle Co., IL

Children of EMMA GRUSH and JOHN ARNOLD are:
    i. BENJAMIN ABNER[6] ARNOLD, b. January 28, 1862, Ogle Co., IL; d. November 24, 1932, Freeport, Stephenson Co., IL.
   ii. ALBERT J. ARNOLD, b. September 07, 1866, Ogle Co., IL; d. March 24, 1938, East Moline, Rock Island Co., IL; m. LILLIE ANN COFFMAN, June 15, 1893, Rochelle, Flagg Twp., Ogle Co., IL; b. December 15, 1867, Lincoln Twp., Ogle Co., IL; d. April 07, 1900.

       Notes for ALBERT J. ARNOLD:
       Illinois Deaths and Stillbirths Index, 1916-1947

       Name: Albert J Arnold
       Birth Date: 7 Sep 1866
       Birth Place: Mount Morris, , Ill
       Death Date: 24 Mar 1939
       Death Place: East Moline, Rock Island, Ill
       Burial Date: 27 Mar 1939
       Burial Place: Polo, Ogle, Ill
       Cemetery Name: Local
       Death Age: 72
       Occupation: Teacher
       Race: White
       Marital Status: M
       Gender: Male
       Residence: Freeport, Stephenson, Ill
       Father Name: John Arnold
       Father Birth Place: U.S.
       Mother Name: Emma Grush
       Mother Birth Place: PA.
       Spouse Name: Mary Arnold
       FHL Film Number: 1819609

       More About ALBERT J. ARNOLD:
       Burial: Fairmount Cemetery, Polo, Buffalo Twp., Ogle Co., IL

       More About LILLIE ANN COFFMAN:
       Burial: Fairmount Cemetery, Polo, Buffalo Twp., Ogle Co., IL

   iii. WILLARD D. ARNOLD, b. 1872, Ogle Co., IL; d. 1935; m. FLORA ELIZABETH JACOBS, November 21, 1895, Chicago, Cook Co., IL; b. March 30, 1870, IL; d. 1950.

       More About WILLARD D. ARNOLD:
       Burial: Greenwood Memorial Terrace, Spokane, Spokane Co., WA

       More About FLORA ELIZABETH JACOBS:
       Burial: Greenwood Memorial Terrace, Spokane, Spokane Co., WA

   5. CATHERINE[5] GRUSH (ISAAC[4], PHILIP[3], CHRISTOPHER[2], JOSEPH[1]) was born August 15, 1842 in Shirleysburg, PA, died 15, 1936 Mason City, Cerro Gordo Co., Iowa. She married Jesse Palmatier on December 31, 1864. He was born Aug. 8, 1830 and died Feb. 4, 1918.

Children of Catherine Grush and Jesse Palmatier are:
>   Henriette Palmatier 1865-1949
>   Marcus Jesse b. Jul. 2, 1870 d. Jul. 15, 1964
>   Bitha C Palmatier 1873-1929

More about Catherine Grush Palmatier:
Residence: 1850, Pine Creek, Ogle, Illinois; 1870, Deep River, Poweshiek, Iowa; 1900, Thornburg Town, Keokuk, Iowa; 1920 and 1930, Prairie, Keokuk, Iowa. Burial: Sixteen Cemetery, Thornburg, Keokuk County, Iowa

More about Jess Palmatier: He was the son of John PALMATEER and Elizabeth (WEAVER) and he came to Ogle County from Delaware County New York sometime after 1850 and before 1855, yet cannot be found in Ogle County in the 1860 census

More about Marcus Jesse Palmatier:
Born in Dresden, Iowa, USA on 2 Jul 1870 to Jesse Palmatier and Catherine Grush. Marcus Jesse married Ella B Johnson (1876-1953) and had 3 children, Clare J Palmatier, Sylvia Palmatier, Gail Perry Palmatier (1907-1967). He passed away on 15 Jul 1964.

    5.   HARRIET[5] "HATTIE" GRUSH (ISAAC[4], PHILIP[3], CHRISTOPHER[2], JOSEPH[1]) b. August 13, 1846 in Ogle Co., IL; d. February 17, 1860.in Ogle CO., IL. Her death was described as being from "consumption."

    5.   DAVID ROLAND[5] GRUSH (ISAAC[4], PHILIP[3], CHRISTOPHER[2], JOSEPH[1]) was born August 05, 1850 in Ogle Co., IL (appears in 1880 Pine Creek Twp., Ogle Co., IL and 1900 Falls City, Richardson Co., NE census), and died February 11, 1928 in Falls City, Richardson Co., NE. He married (1) MARY ANN SNYDER November 23, 1870 in Ogle Co., IL, daughter of JACOB SNYDER and REBECCA KESSELRING. She was born April 08, 1852 in PA, and died April 26, 1873. He married (2) SARAH ELIZABETH SNYDER December 03, 1874 in Ogle Co., IL, daughter of JACOB SNYDER and REBECCA KESSELRING. She was born November 03, 1857 in PA, and died September 10, 1924.

More About DAVID ROLAND GRUSH:
Burial: Steele Cemetery, Falls City, Richardson Co., NE

More about Mary Ann Snyder Grush:
Born April 8, 1852 in Newton, Hamilton, Pennsylvania
or Born in Ogle, Illinois, USA on 1852 to Jacob C Snyder and Rebecca Kesselring
Mary Ann married David Roland Grush and had 2 children.
She passed away on 26 Apr 1873 in Ogle, Illinois, USA

More about Sarah Elizabeth Snyder Grush:
Born in Newton Hamilton, Mifflin, Pennsylvania, USA on 11 Mar 1857 to Jacob C Snyder and Rebecca Kesselring.Sarah Elizabeth married David Roland Grush and had 8 children.
She passed away on 9 Oct 1924 in Falls City, Nebraska, USA

More about Jacob C. Snyder:
Born in Penn Valley, Pennsylvania, USA on 13 Jan 1823 to Nicholas Schneider and Maria. Jacob C married Rebecca Kesselring on 05 Mar 1846 in Newton Hamilton, Mifflin Co PA. and had 11 children. He passed away on 7 Dec 1903 in Salem, Richardson, Nebraska, USA.

More About Rebecca Kesselring:
Rebecca Kesselring was born 03 May 1825, and died 25 Feb 1910 in Salem, Richardson County NE. She married Jacob C Snyder on 05 Mar 1846 in Newton Hamilton, Mifflin Co PA, son of Nicholas Schneider and Maria. Religion: Dunkard Brethern Church.

Children of DAVID GRUSH and MARY SNYDER are:
    i.   DAVID LOUIS[4] GRUSH, b. September 17, 1871, Ogle Co., IL; d. July 03, 1933.

        More About DAVID LOUIS GRUSH:
        Burial: Maple Cemetery, Salem, Richardson Co., NE

   ii. WILLIAM HENRY GRUSH, b. April 17, 1873, Ogle Co., IL; d. July 16, 1953.

        More About WILLIAM HENRY GRUSH:
        Burial: Steele Cemetery, Falls City, Richardson Co., NE

Children of DAVID GRUSH and SARAH SNYDER are:
   iii. CHARLES DALLAS[4] GRUSH, b. November 29, 1875, IL; d. May 28, 1944.

        More About CHARLES DALLAS GRUSH:
        Burial: Steele Cemetery, Falls City, Richardson Co., NE

   iv. ELMER GRUSH, b. Abt. 1879, IL.
   v. AUSTIN GRUSH, b. July 15, 1882, IL; d. May 16, 1924.

        More About AUSTIN GRUSH:
        Burial: Steele Cemetery, Falls City, Richardson Co., NE

   vi. LLOYD B. GRUSH, b. February 21, 1885, IL; d. November 21, 1950.

        More About LLOYD B. GRUSH:
        Burial: Steele Cemetery, Falls City, Richardson Co., NE

   vii. LULU MARY GRUSH, b. September 02, 1891, IL; d. September 19, 1959.

        More About LULU MARY GRUSH:
        Burial: Steele Cemetery, Falls City, Richardson Co., NE

   viii. JESSE HOWARD GRUSH, b. January 04, 1894, NE; d. January 28, 1971.

        More About JESSE HOWARD GRUSH:
        Burial: Steele Cemetery, Falls City, Richardson Co., NE

   ix. INA REBECCA GRUSH, b. November 15, 1895, NE; d. May 28, 1946, Freeport, Stephenson Co., IL; m. ALVA WILFORD DUNN; b. 1876; d. 1947.

        Notes for INA REBECCA GRUSH:
        Illinois Deaths and Stillbirths Index, 1916-1947

Name: Ina Rebecca Grush Dunn
[Ina Rebecca Grush Grush]
Birth Date: 15 Nov 1895
Birth Place: Fall City, Nebraska
Death Date: 28 May 1946
Death Place: Freeport, Stephenson, Illinois
Burial Date: 31 May 1946
Burial Place: Florence Township, Stephenson, Illinois
Cemetery Name: Oakland
Death Age: 50
Occupation: Housewife
Race: White
Marital Status: M
Gender: Female
Residence: Freeport, Stephenson, Illinois
Father Name: David R. Grush
Father Birth Place: PA.
Mother Name: Sarah Snyder
Mother Birth Place: PA.
Spouse Name: Alva W. Dunn
FHL Film Number: 1991308

More About INA REBECCA GRUSH:
Burial: Oakland Cemetery, Freeport, Stephenson Co., IL

More About ALVA WILFORD DUNN:
Burial: Oakland Cemetery, Freeport, Stephenson Co., IL

   x. MABEL GRUSH, b. September 13, 1897, NE; d. August 24, 1980; m. EVAN H. MORRIS; b.
April 06, 1900; d. October 16, 1987.

      More About MABEL GRUSH:
      Burial: Pleasant Hill Cemetery, Richardson Co., NE

      More About EVAN H. MORRIS:
      Burial: Pleasant Hill Cemetery, Richardson Co., NE

Generation No. 6

   6. JAMES E.[6] GRUSH (PHILIP[5], ISAAC[4], PHILIP[3], CHRISTOPHER[2], JOSEPH[1]) was born October 1861
in IL (appears in 1900 Brookville Twp., Ogle Co., IL census, moved to KS). He married MARGARET
"MAGGIE" E. FAGER December 26, 1886 in Brookville Twp., Ogle Co., IL, daughter of CONRAD FAGER
and MARY MYERS. She was born November 26, 1862 in Brookville Twp., Ogle Co., IL.

More About JAMES EDWARD GRUSH:
Burial: Wichita Park Cemetery, Wichita, Sedgwick Co., KS

More About MARGARET "MAGGIE" ELIZABETH FAGER:
Burial: Wichita Park Cemetery, Wichita, Sedgwick Co., KS

Child of JAMES GRUSH and MARGARET FAGER is:

  i. BLANCHE F.[5] GRUSH, b. April 1889, IL; d. 1975; m. FRANK GARFIELD WHITE, 1916; b. December 1881, IA; d. 1930.

    More About BLANCHE F. GRUSH:
    Burial: Wichita Park Cemetery, Wichita, Sedgwick Co., KS

    More About FRANK GARFIELD WHITE:
    Burial: Wichita Park Cemetery, Wichita, Sedgwick Co., KS

 6. HATTIE EMMA[6] GRUSH (JOHN B.[5], ISAAC[4], PHILIP[3], CHRISTOPHER[2], JOSEPH[1]) was born March 05, 1866 in Polo, Buffalo Twp., Ogle Co., IL, and died October 09, 1943 in Belvidere, Boone Co., IL. She married WILLIAM EDMUND HORNER December 10, 1885 in Polo, Buffalo Twp., Ogle Co., IL, son of PETER HORNER and WILHELMINA BIESECKER. He was born May 30, 1861 in Lanark, Carroll Co., IL (appears in 1910 and 1930 Rock Creek Twp., Carroll Co., IL census), and died January 10, 1940 in Lanark, Carroll Co., IL.

Notes for HATTIE EMMA GRUSH:
Illinois Deaths and Stillbirths Index, 1916-1947

Name: Hattie Horner
[Hattie Grush]
Birth Date: 4 Mar 1865
Birth Place: Stratford, Illinois
Death Date: 8 Oct 1943
Death Place: Belvidere, Boone, Illinois
Burial Date: 12 Oct 1943
Burial Place: Lanark, Carroll, Illinois
Cemetery Name: Lanark
Death Age: 78
Race: White
Marital Status: W
Gender: Female
Residence: Lanark, Carroll, Ill.
Father Name: John Grush
Spouse Name: C. E. Horner
FHL Film Number: 1983538

More About HATTIE EMMA GRUSH:
Burial: Lanark Cemetery, Lanark, Rock Creek Twp., Carroll Co., IL

More About WILLIAM EDMUND HORNER:
Burial: Lanark Cemetery, Lanark, Rock Creek Twp., Carroll Co., IL

Children of HATTIE GRUSH and WILLIAM HORNER are:

  i. CLAUDE ALBERT[7] HORNER, b. February 1887, IL (appears in 1910 Rock Creek Twp., Carroll Co., IL census); d. January 20, 1945, Rockford, Winnebago Co., IL; m. BESSIE L. CROUSE; b. March 1887, WI; d. September 05, 1929, Rockford, Winnebago Co., IL.
  ii. RALPH RAYMOND HORNER, b. March 22, 1893, Lanark, Carroll Co., IL (appears in 1930 Lima Twp., Carroll Co., IL census); d. February 17, 1973, Seattle, King Co., WA.

6. ALEXANDER JAMES[6] GRUSH (JOHN B.[5], ISAAC[4], PHILIP[3], CHRISTOPHER[2], JOSEPH[1]) was born July 14, 1869 in Ogle Co., IL (appears in 1900 Pine Creek Twp., Ogle Co., IL census), and died April 01, 1945 in Aurora, Kane Co., IL. He married IDA BIRDELLEN TOMS November 09, 1893 in Ogle Co., IL, daughter of CHARLES TOMS and MARY WOLTZ. She was born March 01, 1874 in Ogle Co., IL, and died May 05, 1965 in Aurora, Kane Co., IL.

L to R: Alex Grush, Madeline Grush, Ida B. Grush,
Vernon Grush holding daughter Suzanne, and on steps Byron Grush, Sr.

Notes for ALEXANDER JAMES GRUSH:
Illinois Deaths and Stillbirths Index, 1916-1947

Name: Alexandre James Grush
Birth Date: 14 Jul 1869
Birth Place: Ogle County, Illinois
Death Date: 1 Apr 1945
Death Place: Aurora, Kane, Illinois
Burial Date: 5 Apr 1945
Burial Place: Naperville, DuPage, Illinois
Cemetery Name: Naperville
Death Age: 75
Occupation: Oil Dealer
Race: White
Marital Status: M
Gender: Male
Father Name: John B. Grush
Mother Name: Mary Tennis
Spouse Name: Ida Birdellen
FHL Film Number: 1984186

More About ALEXANDER JAMES GRUSH:
Burial: Naperville Cemetery, Naperville, DuPage Co., IL
(see Appendix L, "The Alexander Grush Family")

More About IDA BIRDELLEN TOMS:
Burial: Naperville Cemetery, Naperville, DuPage Co., IL

Obit Birdellen Grush:
Dies at Age 91
Birdellen Grush, widow of the late Alexander J. Grush, former mayor of Naperville, died Wednesday, May 5th at the age of 91. She was born March 1, 1874 near Polo, Illinois. Funeral services were held Friday in the First United Methodist church, with Rev. Theodore Potter officiating. Interment was in Naperville cemetery. She was a member of the First United Methodist church and of the Daughters of the American Revolution. In addition, she was a past worthy Matron of the Order of the Eastern Star, and a past Noble Grand of the Floral Rebekah lodge. Surviving are two sons; Vernon of Downers Grove and Byron of Naperville; eight grandchildren and 16 great-grandchildren. [Submitted by Byron Grush, transcribed by Kris Dunlap]

More About IDA BIRDELLEN TOMS:
Her parents were Charles E. Toms and Mary Elizabeth Woltz.

Charles E. Toms

Charles E. TOMS b: April 20, 1837 in Boonsboro, Washington Co., MD (appears in 1870, 1880 and 1900 Pine Creek Twp., Ogle Co., IL census) d: August 28, 1915 in Ogle Co., IL Burial: Pine Creek Brethren Cemetery, Pine Creek Twp., Ogle Co., IL

Mary Elizabeth WOLTZ b: May 29, 1842 in Washington Co., MD m: October 26, 1865 in Ogle Co., IL d: June 13, 1922 Burial: Pine Creek Brethren Cemetery, Pine Creek Twp., Ogle Co., IL Father: James Walling Wolz Mother: Louisa Amelia Petrie

Ida Birdellen Toms was a descendant of Major John George Adam Wolz who fought in the American Revolutionary War. She was a member of the Daughters of the American Revolution.

From: The Wolz Family
By Flora Lee Wolz
Copyright November, 1930

Second edition, May, 1949

…the direct line of descent of Dr' Peter Wolz and his brother Major John George Adam Wolz. [American Revolutionary War]

1. FREDERICK REINHART WOLZ, according to Rupp's "Thirty Thousand Immigrants" -(Vol 17., 2nd Ser. Penn Arc.) was the first man by that name to come to America.
… He first settled in Pennsylvania…. We soon find him however among the settlers of Northern Maryland…. Frederick County, Maryland was erected in 1782, and here is where Frederock R. Wolz settled and where he died in 1782.

2. JOHN PETER WOLZ, eldest son of Frederick Rhinehart Wolz and Charity ( ) Wolz was born in 1719 and came to this county in 1738, on the "Charming Nancy", from Rotterdam. (See Straus burger's "Pennsylvania German pioneers, page 246). He was married 1744-11-24 to Maria Elizabeth Hasin (Haas). She was born 1722-12-10; died 1789-5-4. (See Hist. Soc. Rec. of York, PA..) …John Peter Wolz was a Physician in Berkeley County, Virginia (Now West Virginia).

[Major John George Adam Wolz was one of five children of Dr. Peter (Sr.) and Elizabeth (Haas).]
[p. 67] Major John George Adam Wolz …was the son of Dr. Peter Wolz Sr., and his wife Maria Elizabeth Haas (Hasin). The records of the Christ Lutheran Church of York, PA., state that he was born 1744-10-16…. He was married 1769-2-10 to Charlotte Shugers (b. 1751-7-12; d 1820-3-22). Maj. Wolz was by trade a cabinet make of Hagerstown, Md….

In Part I, page 19, of the "Revolutionary Records of Maryland" by Brumbaugh, is given a list of 271 names of the people who had taken the Oath of Fidelity in Obedience to an act of assembly by the State of Maryland. It is entitled "The Worshipful Henry Schnebley's Returns". We find the names of George and Peter Wolz on the list.

The proceedings of Maryland, held at the City of Annapolis in 1776, page 79, state that George Wolz was 2nd Major in the First Battalion of the Frederick County Maryland Militia, 1776.

The Toms Family:
Mary Woltz Toms, Ida B. Toms Grush, Charles E. Toms holding Vernon Grush(?)

From:
Application For Membership
Sons of the Revolution in the State of Illinois

By Vernon Charles Grush

1. ...[VERNON CHARLES GRUSH] ...was born on January 4, 1896 in Oregon, Ill....

2. ...he is the son of ALEXANDER JAMES GRUSH Born in Ogle Co. Ill on July 14, 1870, died in Aurora, Ill on April 1, 1944 and BIRDELEN TOMS his wife, born in Mt. Morris, Ill on March 1 1876 ..., married in Ogle Co. Ill on July 14 1894.

3. ...BIRDELLEN TOMS was the daughter of CHARLES EDWARD TOMS born... on April 20 1840, died in Ogle Co., Ill ... and MARY ELIZABETH WOLZ his wife, born in Hagerstown, Md on May 23 1842, died in Polo, Ill ... married on October 26 1865.

4. ...MARY ELIZABETH WOLZ was the daughter of JAMES WILLIAM WOLZ born in Hagerstown, Md on Sept 9, 1817, died in Ogle Co. Ill on May 26 1889 and Louisa Amelia Petrie his wife born... on March 6, 1822, died... April 10, 1896,... married on Dec 31 1838.

5. ...JAMES WILLIAMS WOLZ was the son of GEORGE (ELIE) WOLZ born in Hagerstown, Md on May 7 1789, died in Hagerstown, Md on May 19, 1858, and Eliza Gregg Walling his wife born... Sept 23, 1797, died in (will recorded in Hagerstown) May 2, 1867, married... on July 2 1816.

6. ...GEORGE (ELIE) WOLZ was the son of MAJOR [JOHN] GEORGE ADAMS WOLZ born in York, Pa on Oct 16, 1744, died ...June 15, 1813, and Charlotte Shugars his wife born... July 12, 1751, died... March 22, 1820, married in Hagerstown, Md on February 10, 1769.

7. ...MAJOR [JOHN] GEORGE ADAMS WOLZ was the son of DR> PETER WOLZ, SR, born in Rotterdam, Germany [?] on 1719, died in Berkley Co., Va [W. VA]... and Maria Elizabeth Haas his wife, born... Dec 10, 1722 died... May 4 1789, married in York, Pa on Nov 24 1743.

Children of ALEXANDER GRUSH and IDA TOMS are:
    i. VERNON CHARLES[7] GRUSH, b. January 04, 1896, IL; d. April 29, 1968, Downers Grove, DuPage Co., IL. m. Madelyn Coombs, b. May 6, 1898, d. Feb 5, 1998, daughters: Suzanne Crow, Rosemary Vocke, Jane Behrel

More About VERNON CHARLES GRUSH:
Burial: Naperville Cemetery, Naperville, DuPage Co., IL

1968-04-30 Chicago Tribune (IL) Vernon Grush Edition: Chicago Tribune
Services for Vernon Grush, 72, former vice president of Arrow Tool company, will be held at 9:30 a.m. tomorrow in the chapel at 4920 Main St., Downers Grove. Mr. Grush, who lived at 1346 Turney rd., Downers Grove, died Sunday in Hinsdale hospital. He recently retired from the tool company here, where he had been employed for 20 years. Surviving are his widow, Madelyn; three daughters, Mrs. Suzanne Crow, Mrs. Rosemary Vocke, and Mrs. Jane Behrel; 11 grandchildren; and a brother. Record # 19680430ob006

Vernon Grush served in world War I as an ambulance driver for WWI Base Hospital 13 in Limoges France and appears on the Naperville World War I Honor Role. (see Appendix M)

Children of VERNON CHARLES[7] GRUSH and Madelyn LaCharty Coombs are:
    i.   Suzanne (Grush) Crow (April 22, 1921 - December 16, 2011)

More About Suzanne Grush Crow:
Suzanne G. Crow, 90, of Sister Bay, Wisconsin, left her body on Friday, December 16, at home with her children at her side.

Suzanne was born April 22, 1921 in Oak Park, Illinois to Vernon Charles and Madelyn DeCharty Grush. She grew up in Downers Grove, Illinois with two sisters, Rosemary and Jane. She was thankful for her early years at The Avery Coonley School, which she felt started her on the path of lifetime learning.

In 1943, Suzanne enlisted in the US Navy, serving as an Aviation Machinists Mate Third Class. While stationed in Atlanta she met and, after a short courtship, married Army 2nd Lieutenant William Evans Crow II on December 4, 1944. Suzanne and Bill had 4 children: Peter, Patty, Billy and Mark.

Suzanne was a homemaker with a variety of passions including archeology, geology, Colonial American antiques, entertaining, and painting in watercolors. Her collection of Native American artifacts and mineral specimens are bequeathed to The Avery Coonley School. Mother/Daughter, an exhibit of watercolors by Suzanne and Patricia Crow is currently on display at the UU Gallery in North Ephraim. Suzanne's "last hurrah" was the exhibit's opening reception on December 2, when she was able to entertain family, friends and mentors one last time.

Suzanne and her husband Bill moved to Door County in 1999, drawn by the natural beauty and golf courses. She played with the Peninsula State Park's Ladies and Odd-Couples Golf Groups as well as Maxwelton Braes' Bonnie Braes. It was a sad time when her "bum" shoulder ended her golfing career at 86.

Suzanne was preceded in death by her parents, sister Rosemary, husband, and children Peter and Mark. Sister, Jane Behrel of Downers Grove, Illinois, daughter, Pat Crow of Sister Bay, and son, Bill Crow of Grand Junction, Colorado survive her.

The family wishes to thank Dr. Rebhan, Unity Hospice, Casperson Funeral Home and the Unitarian Universalist Fellowship of Door County for their loving kindness. A celebration of Suzanne's life is planned for some time in the spring

ii.   Rosemary (Grush) Vocke

        More about Rosemary Grush:
        Rosemary Vocke (Grush)
        Birth: August 6, 1923
        Hinsdale, DuPage County, Illinois, United States
        Death: December 6, 2005 (82)
        Hagerstown, Washington County, Maryland, United States
        Immediate Family:
        Daughter of Vernon Charles Grush and Madelyn LaCharty Grush
        Wife of Frederick L. Vocke

iii.   Jane Burrell (Grush) Behrel, b. 1932, m. H. Gordon Behrel

        More about Jane Grush:

…For 100 years, the Behrel Family has celebrated Christmas in a glorious white house on Maple Avenue, in Downers Grove. Jane and her husband Gordon moved into that house in

1961, and she still lives there surrounded by memories of a beautiful life.

If you don't know Jane, then your experience at St. Andrews is incomplete. She's been a member since she was 8 years old. She was baptized and confirmed here. St Andrews is where, in 1952, she was married, and where her 4 children were baptized. She was head of the alter guild for many years, and, as if that weren't enough, she taught Sunday School. Former Rector, Jim Leswing, summed it up best when he was visiting Jane at the Hospital a few years ago. She was critically ill, but he assured the family that she would be fine; she would recover fully. When the family asked how he knew this (I'm sure they thought he was relating a direct message from above), he told them that if anything happened to her, St. Andrew's would simply shut down.

Jane's giving spirit isn't limited to our beloved Church. For over 30 years she volunteered at Little Friends, an organization based in Naperville that serves children and adults with autism and other developmental disabilities. Not only is Jane the hands and feet of Christ, but she's also the heart and soul of St. Andrews.
——http://www.saintandrewschurch.net/jane-behrel/ Date: 30 Jun 2015

More about H. Gordon Behrel:

H. Gordon Behrel, age 87. Long time resident of Downers Grove, member of Chicago Board of Trade since 1948. Served in WWII, participating in the Battle of Lete. Beloved Son of Will Roy and Katherine, nee Kearney; loving husband for 56 years of Jane, nee Grush; devoted father of Kathie (Richard) Warner, William, Christopher, David (Kristin); beloved grandfather of Amy (Rob) Salistean, Andrew Warner, Emily, Bryan, Will; and adored great-grandfather of Ayla Jane Salistean. A private memorial will be held at St. Andrews in Downers Grove, Friday. In lieu of flowers, memorials to Tribune Charities.
——Published in a Chicago Tribune Media Group Publication on Mar. 26, 2010

ii. SHIRLEY BEATRICE[7] GRUSH, b. September 1899, IL. m. Homer Boelter.

More about Shirley Grush:
Birth: 4 Sep 1899 in Pine Creek Township, Ogle County, Illinois
Death: 26 Oct 1953 in Los Angeles County California
Burial: Inglewood Park Cemetery, Inglewood, Los Angeles County, California, USA
Plot: Mausoleum of the Golden West, Sanctuary of Fidelity

More about Shirley Grush Boelter:
1940 census for Shirley B Boelter
Age 41, born abt 1899
Birthplace   Illinois
Gender   Female
Race   White
Home in 1940
5112 Deane Avenue
Venice,
Los Angeles, California
Household Members   Age
Head   Homer H Boelter   42
Wife Shirley B Boelter   41
Son Donald E Boelter   15
Son Herbert Boelter 8

More about Homer H. Boelter:
He had a lithography business and was a publisher.
Name: Homer Herman Boelter
Gender: Male
Birth Date: 9 Feb 1899
Birth Place: Minnesota, United States of America
Death Date:19 Jan 1977
Death Place: Los Angeles County, California, United States of America
Cemetery: Inglewood Park Cemetery
Burial or Cremation Place: Inglewood, Los Angeles County, California
Family Members
Parents
August John Boelter
1871–1960
Ada M. Beidelman Boelter
1877–1934
Spouses
Shirley Beatrice Grush Boelter
1899–1953
Ercelle Marguerite Scott Boelter
1907–1976
Children
Donald Eugene Boelter
1924–2001

    iii.   BYRON EDWARD[7] GRUSH (SR), b. July 28, 1908 in Naperville, DuPage Co., IL, d. Feb. 24, 1984. m. Olga Marion Olson, b. April 21, 1912, d. Dec 15, 2002, children: James Alexander, Byron E. Grush, Jr., Mary Ellen.

More about Byron E. Grush Sr.:
GRUSH Byron E. Grush Sr., beloved husband of Olga; dear father of James A., Byron E. Jr. (Martha) and Mary Ellen; loving grandfather of five; preceded by brother, Vernon and sister Shirley. Services Tuesday, 10:30 a m, Beidelman-Kunsch Funeral Home, 117 W. Van Buren Ave. Naperville. Interment Naperville Cemetery. Visitation Monday, 1 to 9 p.m. Memorials may be made to the Heart Fund. into. 355 0264.
      ——Chicago Tribune

(see Appendix L, The Family of Alexander James Grush)

More about Olga Marion Olson:
When Olga Marion Olson was born on 21 April 1912, in Superior, Douglas, Wisconsin, United States, her father, John Olson, was 35 and her mother, Johanna Sophia Swenson, was 35. She lived in Douglas, Wisconsin, United States in 1920 and Naperville, DuPage, Illinois, United States in 1940. She died on 15 December 2002, at the age of 90, and was buried in Naperville, DuPage, Illinois, United States.

Olga Grush of Naperville A memorial service for Olga Grush, 90, will be held at 11 a.m. Saturday, at Beidelman-Kunsch Funeral Home, 516 S. Washington St., Naperville. Born April 21, 1912, in Superior, Wis., she died Sunday, Dec. 15, 2002, at Edward Hospital in Naperville. Interment will be private. Mrs. Grush taught English at North Central College and was a Champion Masters Swimmer. She was a member of the First Congregational United Church of Christ in Naperville and was an artist and a writer. She is survived by her sons, James of Naperville and Byron (Martha) of Cerrillos, N.M.; daughter, Mary Grush of Los Altos, Calif.;

five granddaughters; and one great-granddaughter [?]. She was preceded in death by her parents, John and Sophie (nee Swenson) Olson; husband, Byron E. Grush; and sister, Ellen Brocker [Broecker] of Naperville. Memorials may be made to the American Cancer Society, 999 N. Main St., Glen Ellyn, IL 60137. Friends may visit www.dailyherald.com/obits to express condolences and sign the guest book. For funeral information, (630)355-0264 or www.beidelmankunschfh.com.

——Published in Chicago Suburban Daily Herald on December 18, 2002

(see Appendix O, early photo and Trip to Sweden in 1970)

Parents
John Olson 1876–1940, born in Sweden
Johanna Sophia Swenson 1876–1944, born in Sweden
Residence: Superior, Wisconsin

Siblings
Olaf Gotifred Fred Olson 1901–Deceased, born in Sweden
Richard Emanuel Olson 1901?–1972, born in Sweden
Ellen W Olson 1905–1975. M. Lester Broeker (1906 – 1984)
    (see Appendix Q)
Edward John Olson 1907–1955
Arthur William Olson 1909–1983
Lillian Olson 1914 - 2004
Clarence Olson 1913-1914

Federal Census 1920 for John Olson:
name: John Olson
residence: Superior, Douglas County, Wisconsin
estimated birth year: 1877
age: 43
birthplace: Sweden
relationship to head of household: Self
gender: Male
race: White
mantal status: Married
father's birthplace: Sweden
mother's birthplace: Sweden
film number: 1821985
digital folder number: 4391500
image number: 00307
sheet number: 11

	Household	Gender	Age
	John Olson	M	43y
spouse	Sophia Olson	F	43y
child	Fred Olson	M	20y
child	Richard Olson	M	18y
child	Ellen Olson	F	14y
child	Edwin Olson	M	12y
child	Arthur Olson	M	9y
child	Olga Olson	F	7y
child	Lillian Olson	F	5y
child	Clarence Olson	M	ly lm

Children of BYRON EDWARD[7] GRUSH (SR) and Olga Marion Olson are:

i. James Alexander Grush
    b. July, 1941 in Aurora, Illinois
    married Marilyn Cook, 2 children, Amaryllis (Grush) Lonsinger and Melissa Grush
ii. Byron Edward[8] Grush (Jr)
    b. November 11, 1943 in Aurora, Illinois
iii. Mary Ellen Grush
    b. October 28, 1947 in Aurora, Illinois
    married Kenneth Takagi Takara, October 25, 1981. 1 child Stephanie Suzanne

More about Byron Edward[8] Grush (Jr):
b. November 11,1943
married to Martha Gale Glennon, November 19, 1966
Children of Byron Edward[8] Grush (Jr) and Martha Gale Glennon are:
    i. Abigail Jane Grush
    ii. Emily Johanna Grush Federighi

More about Martha Gale Glennon Grush:
b. January 25, 1944
parents: William Edward Glennon b. 1913, and Beatrice Jane Pierson (1915 – 2012)

More about Jane Pierson Glennon:
descendant of Samuel Fuller, a passenger on the ship Mayflower in 1620
(see Appendix P: Fuller lineage)

Jane Pierson Glennon was born February 21, 1915, in Pierson, daughter of Beatrice Jane Pierson. She married William Edward Glennon
Surviving are children, Martha (Byron) Grush and John (Lea-Carol) Glennon; grandchildren, David Glennon, Abigail, Grush, Caroline Glennon Goodman, Emily Grush Federighi, Andrew Glennon, Genevieve Glennon and Jennifer Bond Brugge and seven great-grandchildren.
She was preceded in death by her mother; her husband; daughter, Kathryn Ann and sons, David George and Charles Edward.
——Pontiac Daily Leader- 12.02.2012

Appendix A

History of Warwick Township
In 1729, Lancaster County, named after the English Shire (county) of Lancaster, became the fourth division of Pennsylvania, and seventeen townships of Lancaster County were created. Warwick Township was the eleventh township formed of the original seventeen townships of the county. Warwick Township originally included the Townships of Warwick, Elizabeth, Clay and as well as the Borough of Lititz.
https://www.warwicktownship.org/administration/pages/history-of-the-township

Lititz
Lititz grew out of a Moravian settlement that was founded in 1754. However, the town's roots extend back to the 15th century's Bohemian Revolution, whose cause was religious freedom. Despite the demise of its leader, John Huss, in 1415, the revolution's fervor lived on. By 1457, his followers – primarily from Bohemia and Moravia in Czechoslovakia – had found refuge on the estate of the king of Bohemia, whose palace was called Lititz.

In the early 1700s, Count Zinzendorf had become the leader of the movement, which had spread to England and North America. The faithful became knowns as Moravians.

Zinzendorf visited Warwick Township in 1742, which led to plans of building a settlement there. Land was secured in 1754, when John George Klein and his wife donated nearly 500 acres to the church. Building lots were laid out three years later. The settlement was named Litiz (the postmaster added the second "t" a century later).
——https://www.lancastercountymag.com/lititz-keeping-history-alive/

The Lititz Moravian Congregation was organized on February 19, 1749. It was then known as the "Warwick Country Congregation" and included local farmers "awakened" by the preaching of itinerant Moravian ministers. The Moravian motto "In essentials, unity; in non-essentials, freedom; and in all things, love" was appealing to these early settlers in Lancaster County.
——https://www.lititzmoravian.org/about-us/

Appendix B

Descendants of Theodorus Aebi (December 2008)

112. JOEL5 EBY(5) (BENJAMIN4 EBY(4), JACOB3 EBY(3), PETER2 EBY(2), DURST (THEODORUS)1 AEBI(1)) was born 06 Apr 1793 in Leacock Twp. Lancaster, Pennsylvania, and died 28 Mar 1861 in Stephenson County, Illinois. He married ELIZABETH GRUSH Abt. 1818 in Leacock Twp, Lancaster, Pennsylvania. She was born 1794 in Philadelphia, Pennsylvania, and died Abt. 1880 in Piatt County, Illinois.

More About JOEL EBY(5):
Name 2: Joel Ebey
Date born 2: Philadelphia, Pennsylvania

Date born 3: 1792, Philadelphia
Died 2: Prob. Nora, Jo Davies Co., Illinois
Burial: Chelsea Breth. Cemetery Lena, Illinois
Residence 1: 1860, Nora, Jo Daviess, Illinois
Residence 2: 1850, Buffalo, Ogle, Illinois

Notes for ELIZABETH GRUSH:
Living with son Joel R. Eby in Oakley, Macon, Illinois in 1880

Children of JOEL EBY(5) and ELIZABETH GRUSH are:

i.	AGNES6 EBY(6).
ii.	CATHERINE EBY(6).
iii.	HENRY EBY(6).
iv.	JACOB EBY(6).
v.	MARY EBY(6).
vi.	SARAH EBY(6).
vii.	SOLOMON EBY(6).
viii.	DAUGHTER EBY(6), b. Abt. 1815.
ix.	WILLIAM EBY(6), b. Mar 1816, Pennsylvania.
x.	DAUGHTER EBY(6), b. Abt. 1818.
xi.	GEORGE W. EBY(6), b. 1819, Philadelphia, Pennsylvannia; d. Aft. 1860.
xii.	JOHN EBY(6), b. 08 Sep 1820, Huntingdon, Co., Pennsylvania; d. 22 May 1899, Hartington, Cedar Co, Nebraska.
xiii.	PHILLIP G. EBY(6), b. Abt. 1822, Pennsylvania; d. Aft. 1880.
xiv.	BENJAMIN EBY(6), b. 1826, Pennsylvania.
xv.	DAVID EBY(6), b. Abt. 1827, Philadelphia, Pennsylvannia.
xvi.	MOSES EBY(6), b. 1829, Pennsylvania.
xvii.	JESSE EBY(6), b. Abt. 1836, Philadelphia, Pennsylvannia.
xviii.	JOEL R. EBY(6), b. Abt. 1841, Philadelphia, Pennsylvannia; d. Aft. 1930, probably Illinois; m. VIRGINIA ----; b. Abt. 1852, Ohio; d. Bef. 1930.
xix.	ELIZABETH EBY(6), b. 1848, Illinois.

Beaumont, Texas, Oct. 21, 1909.

Mr. Chas. H. Welch,

Dear Sir.*—Your letter received. I will give you a short history of the owners of the farms in Germany Valley 64 years ago or in the year 1845. Beginning at the old fullen mill, south of the old stone church: John Young, Philip Grush, Philip Stambaugh, Joseph Kough, David Kough, George Kough. These persons all lived at the old fullen mill. Mathias King on the Blacklog Mountain above Andrew Spanogle farm. Andrew Spanogle farm owned and farmed by Andrew Spanogle, old grandmother Lutz at the Stone Church, Samuel Lutz farm, Jonas Umbenhour at foot of Blacklog Mountain, John Gãrver farm, this farm soon after sold to David Eby, John Wakefield farm, Jacob Lutz farm, Joseph Miller farm, John Long farm, now the Brant farm, Adam Crouse home was not then built, Samuel Rorer farm, Edward Furnace property owned and operated by Samuel H. Bell, Vineyard Mills now called Otelia, owned and occupied by Samuel H. Bell, Oliver Etnier saw mill, S. H. Bell farm occupied by John Price, an Etnier farm occupied by Stephen Elliot and afterward owned by JacobSpanogle great-grandfather of yourself (C. H. Welch.) William Shaeffer farm, Samuel Etnier farm bought in 1844 by my father Thomas A. Smelker, Perry county, Peter Long farm occupied by Benjamin Long afterward sold to Thomas A. Smelker, this Peter Long farm and the Samuel Etnier farm combined have long been known as the Smelker farm, George Eby farm and saw mill afterward the Benjamin Garver farm. Henry Eby fullen mill, George Smith home afterward the Mosey Everet home not yet built, the Richard Hall farm all in timber, the John Etnier farm long known as Johnstown on the ridge above the Jacob Lutz farm, the George Bowman farm, the Robert Wakefield farm at the Bethel church was in after years made from parts of the George Eby farm and the Bowman farm, the George Swine farm, the old tan yard owned and operated by Thomas A. Smelker, my father, the Abraham Long farm occupied by Jacob Spanogle great-grand-father of C. H. Welch, the Peter Swine farm

.was taken from the Abraham Long farm, David Eby farm now known as Dan Berkstresser farm; then came the old log mill and the T. N. Barton farm which was then owned by David Eby, the county poor farm was then owned by my father Thomas A. Smelker, the Billy McGarvey farm was then in timber, timber was on all the land between where the the old log mill stood and fort run near the old tannery. Much of the land in Germany Valley has been cleared since my early recollection.

Very Respectfully,

C. B. SMELKER.

History

of the

Isaac Grush Family

Back in the sixteenth and seventeenth centuries when the European nations were in the midst of their religious conflicts the Huguenots, or French Protestants, were forced to leave their native country or suffer persecution; so many of them found their way into neighboring countries that were more tolerant of the Protestant faith. Among these folk was a family by the name of DeGrush, or as we know the name, Grush, who went up into Holland, where they stayed until in the eighteenth century when Christopher Grush came to America and settled in Moraviantown (now Littitz), Pennsylvania, in 1735. His wife's name, before marriage, was Kristina Elbe. They had four sons:—Philip, John, David and Christopher.

Philip married a Zentmeier and settled in Pennsylvania. John married a Shafer, settlement unknown. David and Christopher never married.

Philip had three sons:—Isaac, William and James. Also a daughter, Mrs. Ebey, whose last known address was Washington, Iowa.

The first mentioned son, Isaac, became the head of the Grush family, of whom we are especially interested, with a possible one-hundred-sixty-five or more living direct descendants to date, there being over three hundred names on the family tree.

A BRIEF HISTORY OF THE
GRUSH FAMILY

W. E. Bomberger, Gowrie, Iowa

My knowledge of the early history of the Grush family is limited. I can recall many times in my boyhood days when I could have obtained dates and facts that would be valuable now. In our young days we do not seem to care for family history as we do in older life. I do not know of any of the Grushes prior to Isaac Grush, the head of the Grush family that held a reunion in Freeport, Illinois, in June, 1931, and are now making them annual affairs. We are descendents from him directly or indirectly.

His early manhood was spent in Huntingdon County, Pennsylvania. There he married his first wife Catherine. To this union were born six sons and five daughters. Philip and Isaac, twins, John, William, James and David; Mary Jane who married Charles Ayers, Elizabeth, married to Josiah Bomberger, Emma, married to John Arnold, and Catherine, married to Jesse Palmatier. One daughter, Harriet, died at about thirteen years of age.

These facts I have learned from my Mother, gathered from the family Bible, and from my own knowledge of passing events. It seems but yesterday in my memory, but it was away back in the years between 1860 and 1870 that we older children would gather around our sainted Mother's knee in the gathering darkness of the evening and beg her to tell us a story, and good Mother that she was she seldom disappointed us. I realize now that many times her head was probably aching and that her hands and body were weary with the cares of the day.

Our father was a hard working pioneer farmer of Illinois at that time. We were poor but honest and it was hard work to keep the wolf from the door, and yet we never went to bed hungry. Mother's health was not the best in those days, and she had none of the present day conveniences. We had 'running water'—Mother and I carried it from the spring about twenty rods from the house.

The laundry was done on an old-fashioned board right at the spring, to save carrying water. She had a limited education. Newspapers and magazines were a scarce thing in those days, especially in our home, so her stories were naturally of the pioneer times and mostly of her own family doings, which suited us.

I can remember clearly of her telling about her early childhood days in Huntingdon County, Pennsylvania, and about the long drawn-out decision of the family to emigrate to Illinois, where some of their neighbors had already gone, and what an undertaking it was, especially with a large family of small means. Grandfather did not call in a truck and load all his household goods in it, load his family into a new eight-cylinder automobile, honk the horn and start for Illinois. No, he and some of the neighbors who were going with him, went to the Ohio River, not far from Pittsburg, where they built a large raft; then they brought their families and few worldly goods by wagon and loaded all on the raft, loosened the moorings and started on their long weary journey. Nothing to steer or propel the raft but pike poles in the hands of the sturdy mountaineers leaving to become prairie pioneers. For days and days they drifted with the current, aided by the pike poles. Many times they were in great danger in the rapids and swift currents, tying up at night for rest and safety. Finally they reached the great Mississippi River, where they wanted to go up-stream instead of floating. Here they hired a steamboat to pull them up to what is now Savannah, Illinois.

There they were met by some old-time neighbors who had preceded them out West. They came with ox teams and wagons, loaded the goods and women and children in the wagons—the men and boys walking—and thus they started on the last lap of their long trek to the wild prairies of Illinois.

Their journey ended at a point about eight miles east of what is now Polo, Illinois, near Pine Creek. Here a log cabin was hastily erected on land that Grandfather had homesteaded. I was lucky enough to be born in this log cabin about fifteen years later.

I am not quite sure just what year our ancestors landed in Illinois. Mother used to tell us that while being towed up the Mississippi River there was great excitement at Nauvoo when they arrived there. The Mormons were headed for the West. My old encyclopedia tells me that many of the Mormons left Nauvoo in 1845 and that in September, 1846 the balance were driven out, so that our people must have landed in Illinois in either 1845 or 1846. I am inclined to think it was the latter year.

As I stated before, the log house was hastily erected. There were no glass windows available at the time, so the openings were covered with hand woven linen or sheets. The single door was closed in bad weather and at nights by a home-made table set up on end so as to close that hole. This was quite necessary, as at night wild animals would come right up to the house and howl and bark and prowl around. The windows were high in the cabin and small, so there was but little chance for trouble there. Mother would tell us about these depredations of the wild animals. Grandfather and the boys being away working in distant parts of the settlement—for they were earning their living by the sweat of their brows—Grandmother and the younger children would be alone at the cabin. They would have to take the dog into the cabin with them to save his life. They had to build a stockade to protect the cow, the horse, and the hay and other feed. The children did not go out to the movies those nights. Mother told us of many narrow escapes from hungry, half-famished wolves.

One time in particular Grandfather and the older boys had been over at Shellsbers Grove, some six miles south and west, helping to butcher hogs all day and into the night. The settlers in those days marketed their hogs dressed, killing and freezing the carcasses at home and then hauling them to Chicago on home made sleds and getting about the same price that the Iowa farmer did for his hogs under Hoover prosperity. Grandfather had secured a lot of this meat for his family use, and very late he had loaded this meat onto his sled drawn by one faithful horse and he and the boys started for home across the bleak prairie. They had not gone far before they could hear the howl of wolves and soon the hungry horde was upon them. The men tried in vain to scare the wolves off. It seemed that they would attack the wildly running horse or pull the men or meat from the sled in their fury. Something had to be done, so as a last resort the men began throwing off small pieces of the meat. It worked, for the wolves stopped and fought each other until the last scrap of the meat was gone when they resumed the race again, soon overtaking the fleeing sled. Once more the men threw off small pieces of meat, and this was repeated over and over again until they reached home with an exhausted horse and but little pork.

I think it was about the second fall they had been in Illinois that Grandfather made a deal with a neighbor whereby he was to drive a team of oxen with a load of wheat to Chicago and be permitted to bring back some stuff for himself. This was not an easy trip in those days. No graded roads, no bridges, and plenty of wet sloughs. It was the common thing to have to put all the oxen on one load to get it through some of the sloughs, and to even unload some of the wheat and carry it out to higher ground. Grandfather brought some windows and a door for the house and some things for the family. They thought they had a fine house when they got the windows in. I am glad they got the house fixed before I arrived anyway.

Talk about hardships, privations, and real bravery. We of this generation know but little about such things.

I never saw my maternal Grandmother, she having died about eight years before I was born, but I remember Grandfather quite well; in fact, he made his home with us for a while when I was about four or five years old, and then I often visited at his home after he re-married. His second marriage was to a widow lady named Mrs. Eshelman. To this union one child was born, a daughter named Verna. (Mrs. Eshelman had two daughters, Minnie, now Mrs. Nevin Hirsch of Waterloo, Iowa, and Alsie Read of Ottawa, Kansas.)

I take off my hat and bow my head to Isaac Grush, my maternal Grandfather—the grand old pioneer. The soul of honor, his word was worth more than his bond. He did not accumulate money, but he left us a great heritage.

For three generations now I think I can see the blood and character of this grand old man still showing strong. He was a man of but little levity; firm but kind in all his dealings, he commanded great respect. There was no back talk from the children in his home. His children were taught to respect their parents and those above them.

As to the family history of his children I believe that each have children or grandchildren who can do better than I. Except possibly Uncle Jim. Mother told me that he and Uncle John went to California in the mad gold rush, in 1852, and that after great hardships they got through. Then the brothers got separated and

to my knowledge none of his family have ever heard anything from him since. Uncle John had to return without him. In after years much time and money were spent in trying to locate him, but without any results.

———

Grandfather Isaac Grush was born near New Holland, Lancaster County, Pennsylvania, on November 13, 1802, and died in Illinois in 1889 at the age of eighty-seven. He was married to his first wife, Catherine Burns, about the year 1825, in Lancaster County, Pennsylvania and came to Illinois about twenty years later, settling in Buffalo township, near Polo, Illinois. Catherine Grush died October 14, 1851. Several years later Isaac married again, to a Mrs. Catherine Eshelman.

When Isaac Grush brought his family to Illinois by way of the Ohio and Mississippi Rivers he was met at Savannah, Ill., by Sammy Funk, who took him and his family to the Funk home while the new Grush home was being built. The house was built of logs as previously described, and the barn was made of poles covered with hay. Market day came twice a year. Several of the neighbors would go together and drive to the "nearby" city of Chicago, about one-hundred-twenty miles away. Today it means only a few hours drive in a high-powered motor, but driving across country with a team and wagon was no joke, and it took several days to make the trip.

A stage line running from Freeport to Oregon carried mail and passengers. The mail was left at a private home, two miles away. Mrs. Annie Bruebaker was the post-mistress. Postage at that time was five cents a letter.

Perhaps a word about our Grandmother at this time would not be out of place. Catherine Burns Grush was one of nine children, born in Lancaster County, Pennsylvania, June 8, 1806. Her brothers and sisters were Nancy, James, Mary, Milly (known as Aunt Polly Cornelius), Isaac, Sarah (Myers), Jane (Crane) and John. Great-grandmother Catherine Burns lived to be ninety-one years of age, and spent the latter part of her life with her son John at Dresden, Iowa. The Burns family settled at Dresden, Iowa, and several members of the family are buried in the Old Dresden Cemetery, Poweshiek County, Iowa. Great-grandfather Burns died in Pennsylvania.

1 JOHN (1) LATTA

Born: abt. 1750, son of John Latta and Mary Daugherty (See Branch 29 connection). Mary Daugherty/Dougherty's father, Edward Dougherty, owned a tavern in the early 1700's on the Old Conestoga Road outside of Strasburg, Lancaster County, Pennsylvania. John Latta married Mary Nixon, daughter of James and Mary (Potts) Nixon of Brandywine Hundred, Delaware, on January 1, 1773 in New Castle, Delaware. James Nixon was born 1705 in Copaugh, Ireland and died June 26, 1775 in New Castle, Delaware. Mary Potts Nixon was born in 1729 in Clogh, Antrim, Ireland, and died Oct. 29, 1804 in Woodburn, Loudoun County, Virginia. James Nixon is found in New Castle, Delaware in 1731 where he is listed as a cooper, in 1772 as a farmer and in 1773 as a yeoman (freeholder, landowner). The will of James Nixon (found in the Richard Nixon Library) was written May 16, 1773 and probated June 26, 1775. His wife, Mary and son, George, were executors of the will. He stated "To John Latta, my son-in-law and Mary, his wife, L20 in cash." The other children of John and Mary Nixon were James, Catherine, Elizabeth, Jean and a son George Nixon, who was the 4th great-grandfather of President, Richard Nixon. George Nixon, in his pension application for his Revolutionary War service, stated that he served as a soldier who crossed the Delaware and fought in the Battle of Princeton with George Washington.

Revolutionary War Service: John Latta supposedly served as a commissary in the Revolutionary War. He supposedly left his wagon and joined in the fighting and was court martialed, but George Washington dismissed the court martial. (Could this story be for another member of his family. Perhaps Branch 19, John Latta was his grandfather. He supposedly served as a teamster for General Braddock during the French and Indian War, and George Washington took command after General Braddock was killed. This John Latta had a son who died before 1768, as he left part of his estate to the children of his son John. This may have been the John who was killed by Indians (during the French/Indian War) that Latta Grove was named for.)

361 CATHERINE (2) b. abt. 1777, married Isaac Burns about 1799. Isaac Burns was a wheelwright. *History of Huntingdon and Blair Co., by J. Simpson Africa, pg. 345* states "The pioneer wheelwrights of Shirleysburg were ....Isaac Burns, whose shop was between the old John Cooper's tavern and store and Sharrar's cabinet shop." Children: Nancy (b. Apr. 6, 1799); Amelia, (b. June 7, 1804), married Lewis Cornelius, lived in Ogle Co., IL; Mary, (b. Aug. 28, 1802); m Morgan Cornelius; Isaac, Jane, Sarah, (b. Aug. 26, 1796), m. Mr. Crane and lived in Huntingdon Co., PA; James, (b. Nov. 4 1800); Catherine, (b. June 8, 1806), m. Isaac Grush, and lived in Ogle Co., IL; Sarah, (b. July 6 1809) , m. Mr. Myers; and John (b. 1816), m. Elizabeth and lived in Ogle Co., IL. Isaac Burns is listed in the 1800 Census at Shirley over 45, Catherine (26-45), and one daughter under 10. In the 1810 Census, I. Burns is listed at Shirley with his wife, 1 son under 10, 4 daughters under 10, and a daughter 10-16. In the 1820 Census, Isaac and Catherine are at Shirleysburg, and have a son under 10, 1 son 16-26, 1 daughter under 10, 2 daughters 10-16, and 2 daughters 16-26. Catherine and Isaac lived in Shirleysburg until his death between 1820-1830. Catherine is seen in the 1830 at Shirleysburg living with a daughter between the age of 20-30. (This would be Nancy, who never married.) Catherine is listed as age 50-60. In 1840, Catherine is listed as living with her daughter, Mary Cornelius, wife of Morgan Cornelius, in Shirley township. Catherine moved west with her son John Burns and his family in 1849, and is listed in the 1850 census with his family in Ogle County, Illinois. Her daughter, Catherine Grush, wife of Isaac Grush, had moved to Ogle County, Illinois in 1846. (The obituary of her granddaughter, Emma Grush Arnold, stated "In the spring of 1845 she moved with her family westward. They traveled by team and boat on the Ohio River and along the Mississippi to Savanna, Ill., and settled in Ogle County, in Pine Creek Township." The obituary of her grandson, John Grush stated "In 1846 he came west with his parents. They came by boat down the Ohio River and then up the Mississippi to Savanna, then traveled over land on wagons to Pine Creek Illinois." In 1851, Catherine Grush dies. In 1860, Catherine Latta Burns is found in Deep Run, Iowa with her daughter Mary Cornelius' family, and her son John Burns is two houses down. In 1864, Catherine died in 1864 in Dresden, Poweshiek County, Iowa, at the age of 87. She is buried in the Dresden Cemetery, Deep River Township. After her husband passed away, and her father, Catherine traveled west with her children, settling first in Ogle Co., IL, and then in Dresden, Poweshiek County, Iowa, where she died. See obituaries of three of her family members recalling the trip west in 1846.

—— http://www.latta.org/Branches/Branch%2017.htm

Appendix F: The Love Feast

...The lovefeast is primarily a song service, opened with prayer. Often there is no address; the hymns in the ode, or order of service, furnish the subject matter for devotional thoughts. If many visitors are present, the presiding minister often says a few words, explaining the purpose of the service, just before the congregation partakes of the bun and coffee, or whatever is served. On special occasions an address may be added, giving opportunity to remind the congregation of the history of the anniversary or the deeper import of the day.

There is no rule as to the food to be offered, except that it be very simple and easily distributed. The drink may be coffee, tea, or lemonade, fully prepared in advance, so that it may be served very quietly and without interruption of the singing. Usually mugs are used, which may be passed from hand to hand along a pew from a tray brought along the aisle. A slightly sweetened bun, which can be served in baskets passed along the pews, is a convenient form of bread. Usually men handle the trays of mugs, and women the baskets of buns. While the congregation partakes, the choir sings an anthem. Later the mugs are quietly gathered and removed. The food served is not consecrated, as in the communion. Children and members of any denomination may partake.

—— An Excerpt from Customs & Practices of the Moravian Church, Crews & Starbuck, 2003.

Appendix G

Brethren Cemetery, some inscriptions:
http://ogle.illinoisgenweb.org/PineCreekBrethren.txt
Pine Creek Brethren or Dunkard Cemetery, Pine Creek Twp.
Walked and transcribed by Brian E. Hulleberg, May-June 2004
Used with permission on the Ogle US GenWeb Site

Title	Surname	First	Middle	Suffix	Maiden	Day	Month	Year	Day	Month	Year	Notes & inscriptions
Row 9												
	Funk	**Samuel**						1792			1851	Wife - Barbara
	Funk	**Barbara**						1800			1844	"His Wife", husband - Samuel
	Funk	**George**						1826			1842	"Their son"
	Toms	**Charles**	**E.**			20	Apr	1837	28	Aug	1915	Wife - Mary Woltz
	Woltz	**Mary**				29	May	1842	13	Jun	1922	"His Wife", husband - Charles Toms
Row 10												
	Bomberger	**Elizabeth**							10	May	1855	"Wife of Peter Bomberger" & "In the 48th year of her life"
Row 12												
	Sadler	**William**	**H.**					1832			1920	"Commrad 61-65", wife - Elizabeth A.
	Sadler	**Elizabeth**	**A.**					1837			1883	"His Wife", husband - William H.
	Cornelius	**Hattie**	**A.**						9	Feb	1878	"Daughter of J & C Cornelius", death date could be 1828
	Cornelius	**Elias**				15	Oct	1842	26	Dec	1895	Wife - Mary
	Cornelius	**Mary**				23	Mar	1842	4	Jan	1895	"His Wife", husband - Elias
	Grush	**Mary**	**A.S.**									"Wife of David R. Grush"
	Snyder	**Anny**	**B.**									"Daughter of B. Snyder"
	Cornelius	**Amelia**							12	Apr	1852	"Wife of Lewis Cornelius"
	Cornelius	**Lewis**				27	Dec	1797	25	Apr	1881	"Aged 83 Yrs 3 mo & 29 days", wife - Amelia
	Grush	**Isaac**						1802			1890	
	Grush	**Catherine**	**Burns**					1806			1851	
	Grush	**John**	**B.**			22	Sep	1827	22	May	1906	Wife - Mary J. "Gone but not forgotten"
	Grush	**Mary**	**J.**			8	Dec	1835	23	Feb	1870	Husband - John B.

Appendix H
A letter from Philip Eby to William Grush

Found on Cyberbee.com, an educational website using real artifacts in the learning process. Spelling and grammar was not corrected. Punctuation was inserted for easier reading. Origin of letter not cited.

Page 1
Dear Friend, I take this privilege to rite to you that we are able and hope that these few lines may find you in the same state of health. I promised to rite to you as soon as I got to the west but I have neglected it but now I beg your kindness that you will not think hard of it that I did not write to you sooner. I did intend to rite to you as soon as I landed. I had nine days traveling after I left your house and after I got to Rock River I had a severe attack of the bilious fever. I was for three weeks that I was confined to bed but really that did not discourage me of the country we all intend to move to that country this spring. Uncle Isaac Grush is going to move with us to Rock River Settlement. I have got eighty acres of land that I traded the horse and carriage for. I got it for 1.50 cts. per acre. There is many chances yet and first rate Country that a man can make a better liven there then in any Country that I ever was in for they can rais from thirty to fifty bushels to the acre without any expence onely there labour for the land is smooth. I think it is better for at once to leave all and go to Illinois for now is the time to get land cheap for in two years time all the best chances will be taken up for there is many people going to that Rock River Settlement. There is a hundred familys going to from Washington County Maryland. I would like to see you and the family come out next summer to Ogle County Illinois that is the place that we are going to. Isac is going to the same neighborhood. The market was good for to be a new country wheat was seling for seventy five cts per bushel corn twenty cts a bushel when I left that country beef 4 cts per pound pork 5.00 per hundred milch cows from 12 to 15 dollars. I started from Illinois for home on the 20 day of October and landed on the 11 of November. I came by water all the way home.

Page 2
We received a letter from Grand father on the 11 day of February. they is well and like there home. They have moved out to his sisters. David bought him a place in Cambridge but he sa that he will stay where he is for his sister to take care of him as long as he live. Nothin more remains but my love to you and to all the enquiring. Direct your letter Lancaster county Blue Ball Post Office.
I want you to rite me as soon as you received this letter. We intend to start on the 25 of March. Direct your letter to Ogle County Illinois Grand Detour Post Office.
Phillip Eby
Hymn C3 PM is written at the bottom of the page

Page 3
Upper right hand corner: 10
Address:
Mr. William Grush
Galion PO
Richland Co
Ohio
Lower Left Hand Corner
Shade Gap Pa
July unreadable 8th

——http://www.cyberbee.com/primary/Letter/investigation_sites.html

Appendix I
Kingery and Carlock diary entries:

August 5th. This morning quite a number became discouraged as our provisions were running short and the country ahead looked very discouraging. We concluded to abandon the wagons and cut them up to make pack saddles for the horses and cattle, and pack our provisions and such other things as we could. The scene here is hard to describe. Many of the women and children are weeping at the thought of having to leave the wagons and the many things that it would be impossible to pack on the cattle....We at first thought we would do as the others were doing---leave our wagons and pack our cattle---but Mrs. Cook became perfectly frantic at the idea of riding an ox and carry her baby, so we finally concluded to make another effort to get through with our wagons....

Adam Baker Carlock

August 5th Traveld 24 Miles. Road very heavy & rough. Over Sage & Chaperal Stubs or Bushes the ground is very Soft. A Waggon runs Just as it would over ploughed ground. Encamped at Smoke Creek. Water good, grass poor.
Solomon Kingery

August 10th. Traveled up this valley twelve miles and camped at the foot of the Sierra Nevada Mountains....The mountains here are covered with large pine, cedar and fir timber....

Adam Baker Carlock

August 10th   Traveld 15 miles. Road good. Encamped on Smith Creek in the head of Honey lake valy at the foot of the Sierra Nevada Mountain. Grass and water good.

Solomon Kingery

August 11th. Several men went out to guard the cattle, but the supposition is that they all went to sleep and let the Indians kill three head and wound three others; one of the oxen killed belonged to us.

Adam Baker Carlock

August 11th Traveld 17 miles. Commenced ascending the Mt & entered into heavy Pine timber. Road Stony but not Steep. We had to Keep 3 & 4 men ahead of the teams to hunt & Clear the road as there in Some fallen timber in the way. Encamped at the head of a ravine. About 3 Miles down this rivine we found plenty of water & grass. We took the Cattle down with ten or 12 men down to guard them.
Solomon Kingery

August 12th. Several of the men went out on an Indian hunt this morning to revenge the loss of the cattle. They soon found seven of the redskins looking after the cattle they had killed; our men fired and killed three of them; the other four got away.

Adam Baker Carlock

August 12th.Traveld 6 miles. The guards turned the Cattle out to grass. Before daylight this morning the Indians got four of our oxen and out of another team, out to themsleves. Some way and drove them of. As soon as it was light we missed them but it took Soon timeto find the Course that they went with them. 4 of the boys well armed followed them about 2 miles. They found the Cattle: three of them were killed & partly Skind & had a large peice of Stake on a fire Cooking it. They must have heard the boys Coming. The other two oxen had an arrow Shot in each Side. No Indians Could be seen or found near the Cattle. They pulled the arrows out of the Cattle that were Shot & Brought them With them. I think they will both get well. Encamped on a Small Creek. Grass tolerable. We saw Some Indians drive a cow away from here when we Come. 6 of our boys followed them about 6 Miles or near to where they had Killed the other Cattle. They Saw a Smoke in a thicket. Our boys got around on a hill & Killed three of the Indians. 4 more run. They had Killed the Cow and were Cooking Some of the beef.

Solomon Kingery

August 13th. We did not leave camp until noon; them we traveld seven miles to a small lake and camped. This is a fearful hard day's work. The road was very rough and rocky and most of the way was covered with underbrush and large trees had fallen across the trail and which had to be cut out in order for us to pass.

Adam Baker Carlock

August 13th. Traveld 8 miles. Through heavy timber. Encamped on the Lauson rout again at a Small lake. Grass rather poor. This is the best Pine timber I ever Saw.
Solomon Kingery

August 15th. Last night was very dark and as we were afraid the Indians would try to steal some of our stock, we put out a double guard; the night being very cold, the boys started fires in the circle they had formed. My watch came on at twelve o'clock and, as I was passing among the cattle to take my station, I found several of the cattle with Indian arrows sticking into them; none of the arrows had gone deep enough to kill the animals....When we moved on we leaft a few men in camp to see if any of the Indians would come in to get their game. We had scarely gotten out of sight of camp when a big Indian came running into camp; the men shot him down and started on.

Adam Baker Carlock

August 15th   Traveld 20 miles. The Indians Shot 7 oxen for the Company last night again. Only one died; then to day Som of our Company layed in the Bush after the teams left to watch the Indians. After awhile one come up the Creek looking & watching on every Side. When he got within about 100 yards he heard or Seen the boys. He Started & run. Seven of the boys SHot at him. They wounded him. They followed him about one mile; he was still running. They Could easey track him by the blood. We think be bleed to death.
Solomon Kingery

Note for Adam Baker Carlock:

Adam Baker Carlock ventured off to California at the age of nineteen. Henry Wells, in History of Siskiyou County, California, tells us he "started across the plains full of hope and energy, with James Denny and Charles Cook and wife, arriving in Shasta in August, 1852." He had $2.50 in his pocket when he arrived. He began placer mining and accumulated a fair amount of wealth in that way, but tired of it. He then "went to Sacramento with a man named Wilkinson, and bought four mules, which they loaded and began a packing business to Weaverville. Wilkinson soon sold out, and Mr. Carlock formed a partnership with Solomon and Daniel Kingery. In the fall of 1854, the train was divided, and Mr. Carlock continued packing alone till the spring of 1856." Adam Baker Carlock went on to become a prominent banker and served as Senator from 1880 to 1882. Adam Carlock kept a diary of his trip along the Nobles Road. It matches Kingery's as to time and place as they both describe their troubles with Indians, indicating that they both were part of the same wagon train.

Appendix J
Kingery letter to his parents, Shasta City, April 12th, 1853:

Shasta City, April 12th, 1853.

Dear Parents:-

It is with great pleasure that I take my Pen in hand this evening to inform you that I am well, & still more satisfaction that I have just this minute finished reading your letter dated Feby 13th which has been just two month Coming; but we have not received Daniel letter yet, which you say he wrote 2 weeks before you wrote this. I had not got any letter from you for nearly two month. I think you are neglecting to write as often as you agreed. If you Wont letters often you must Write often. I will answer all that you Write, if it is one every Week, or day. Daniel & Harris are Well & are mining on Trinity R., yet, and are Making a living. James Grosh and Wm. Sadler are are at the Same place & are well. I met John Grosh to day Going over on the Trinity from here. He is well and he showed me a letter Which he had just Recd from his father Which I was glad to See, & he also Informed me that he got one from his sister Mary. I Recd a letter from Mr. Wm. Newell about two Weeks ago Which I was indeed glad to Receive. I answered it. I also wrote one to Mr. Hammaker. I am looking for a letter from R. Brubaker. I was glad to hear that Mr. Thos was going to Write for I would like to hear from him very much for I always took him to be a friend to me. I was also very glad to hear that you had a good Meeting & that those have got Religion which you named & that Mr. Neely was your Preacher &c., for I do think that place needed a revival. You did not say what become of Prestninger, but I suppose he must be dead or you would hardly have had a Revival there. If not so, I would advise them to send him to this Country. I think he could get business enough of his own here, without attending to other peoples. You say the report is that we Cal. boys are all homesick; then I suppose you wont be Disappointed if we all get home broke, which may be the Case. It is here like in any new Country; when a person Comes in without any money like me all did & dont know any thing about mining or What to Do, it is discouraging. I think the boys are all pretty well satisfied. Now you say Mr. Stroup is coming [to] Oregon. I think that is a good Country. I am well acquainted with people that live there. I was talking [to a man] from the Umqua Valley to day. He is from Michegan formally. He says it is far ahead of Michegan for raising Wheat or Stock, & the Climate is much Better, I know. But it is a long journey for a family. I have not wrote to Mr. Stroup, as I did not know where to Direct to, as he was talking of leaving there when I left. I am still Packing goods on Trinity River. We

are keeping a little store & doing a tolerable Business. I received two letters from John some time ago,
and answered them. I am looking for one from John
Ayers as I wrote to him in the winter. The coolest
weather we had, a Person could go in his shirt sleeves
here. I am sorry to hear that you had bad luck with
your Buckwheat, for if I could get some now I think
I could store away some Cakes, if not more. I am sorry
to say that we cant send you any money now as we are
using all the money that we have. You can probably
borrow some, as the money is worth more to us here
than three times the interest you would have to pay,
I think. Still, write how you are getting along; we
can probably spare some after a while. I left home
yesterday Morning & got in the City this evening. It
has Commenced to rain since I am Writing. We have no
thunder or lightning here in this Country at all.
This seems strange to me - so much rain without Thunder or lightning. I was glad to hear that grand mother was well & Cousin Leah Balabough. When you Write
to them send my best Respects to them & my address,
for I would like to hear from them. As regards us
geting to be bad boys, we always was pretty bad & we
are a little worse now, I think - if any Difference.
But I heard it said that it was hard to spoil a rot-
ten egg. But does me good to hear that times was getting better. If Stroup is Coming to Oregon you Can
tell him if he will Let me know where he is going I
will Come & see him. I will send paper with this letter. I suppose you will get to see the letter I sent
to Wm Sewel. I saw a California fight a few days ago.
Men do not fight fist fights here like in the States.
They generally fight With pistols. The one I saw, the
one Man got Killed & the other got his leg Broke. I
was not more than Ten feet from them. They quarreled
about Crossing a ferry Just as I was Crossing. They
had pack mules & both wanted to Cross first. Last week
two men fell out here in Town & the one shot the other
Down Dead. The Miners gathered together & hung the other
the next day.
          I will now Close hoping the these few
Lines May find you all well & that you may write soon.
Give My Respects to Mr Grushes family one and all, and
all inquiring persons. I got a letter from Mr Hoisington last week. We will be glad to (hear) from Mr Harve(y)
in your next Letter &c &c.
Market on Trinity River

flour	25 cts per lb	This from your Obedient Son,
Pork	60 " " "	
Bacon	62½ " " "	
Beans	30 " " "	Solomon Kingery
Salt	35 " " "	
Tobacco	1.00 " " "	
D. Apples	45 " " "	to his parents
" Peaches	50 " " "	
Candles	1.00 " " "	
Beef	40, 45 " " "	Daniel & Susannah
Sugar	40 " " "	
Coffee	50 " " "	
Potatoes	30 " " "	Kingery.

- C -

Appendix K, the Indian Wars (so called):

First incident (1854) involving JAMES[5] GRUSH:

From Van Kirk, Susie, "Fort Humboldt Conflict Period" [items from the Humboldt Times]:
(Humboldt Times Editor Edwin D. Coleman 9 Sept. 1854 to 5 Jan. 1856)

HT (23 Sept. 1854) Indian Murder—On Monday morning, the 18th inst., Mr. Arthur Wigmore of St. Louis, Missouri, an Irishman by birth, was killed at the lower Rancheree on Weeott river about a half a mile from his house. A friend writing to us says: "Deceased with three others went to a Rancheree about sunset on Sunday to arrest an Indian who had a few days previously robbed Mr. Hawks' house; they did not find the guilty one and attempted to arrest his father, the Indian resisted and the company were unable to arrest him. Next morning, Monday, the deceased returned to the Rancheree to get a rope he had left there; upon his not returning, on Tuesday, a company went in search of him, when they were informed by some of the Indians that Wigmore was killed and his body thrown into the slough. On Wednesday his friends found his body some distance from the water, where he had been dragged by the Indians. He was shot with a shot gun in the right side, all the back part of his brains were knocked out apparently with an axe; his jugular was cut through, he had 13 other wounds, either of which were mortal. Such was the finding of the jury of citizens, nineteen, who aided in the examination.

An Indian named Billy is charged with having shot Mr. Wigmore, however, there are many stories afloat in regard to the matter. All concur in saying that Mr. Wigmore was a peaceable, industrious, and sober man. The Indians have all fled from their Rancherees into the mountains. On Thursday night the citizens of Eureka held a meeting and passed resolutions, pledging themselves to co-operate with the citizens of the lower end of the county in their endeavors to arrest the supposed murders or punish the tribe. A party went from this place yesterday in pursuit of the Indians, whom they found on the North Beach, they promised to hunt up the murderers of Wigmore and bring them to Eureka, dead or alive. A correspondent asks, "Will those who are vested with authority, paid by the Government, aid in bringing the murderers to justice?".... [microfilm damaged]

Since writing the above, we learn from Mr. Robinson that he and two others on Thursday went up Eel river above the first Fishery and took between twenty and 30 friendly Indians, who came with them and expressed a willingness to assist the white people in arresting the murderers; while with the Indians Mr. Robinson spied a party of nine or ten white man on the opposite side of the river, going toward the Rancheree of some friendly Indians; he wrote a note and dispatched it by an Indian, requesting them to come to him; they received the note and instead of coming to him, pursued their course to the Rancheree, where they commenced shooting the unarmed Indians, two of whom were wounded. Mr. Robinson and companions upon hearing the firing, hastened to the place and induced them to stop shooting. The Indian men ran off, leaving their squaws at the mercy of the white men. One of the men caught a squaw and dragged her across the river, and into the bushes; her screams were heard at some distance. Mr. Robinson finding he could not control the party, left them bringing back his two companions and two of the other party. The balance pursued on after the Indians. The details of the affairs are disgusting.

HT (30 Sept. 1854) The Murderer of Mr. Wigmore Killed—A friend writes us from Eel river, Sunday 24th— "Capt. Pomeas, the chief, and his company have returned from their search after the murderers of Wigmore. They brought the head of one of them they killed last night. I readily recognized his countenance as one of the murderers named by the Indians. They also brought the revolver belonging to the deceased and told where his gun was or could be found, broken. We found the breach but not the barrel. I have the pistol and head in my possession. They are going out again tonight in search of two others they have heard from. We have told them to bring them alive if possible."

HT (30 Sept. 1854) We with pleasure give place to the following contradiction of the statement we published in our last number. Our information was obtained from Mr. Robinson....Eel River, Sept. 27, 1854. Editor of Humboldt Times: We, the company that went in search of the murderers of Wigmore, a few days ago, take this opportunity of informing you that you were misinformed, either malignantly of through ignorance concerning the conduct of said company and particularly as to the committal of violence upon the person of a squaw, by one of our party. G.A. and Thomas Dungan, A. Denman, G.W. Larimore, J.F. Whiten, W. Minor, J. Ripley, James Grush, W.H. Gilman, J.S. Ball.

Second incident (1858) involving JAMES[5] GRUSH:

http://nahc.ca.gov/webmaster/atlas/evidence/i0392.pdf
SACRAMENTO DAILY UNION
LATE FROM NORTHERN CALIFORNIA.
Humboldt Times, of June 12th, gives the following account of the causes of the present difficulties in that region:
On the morning of May 2_tth, a party of eight or ten men went to the rancheria, on Eel River, a few miles above the mouth, and made an attack upon the ranch, killing one Indian and one squaw, and wounding another squaw and a pappoose. The men who made the attack stated that their object was to take some guns which the Indians had in their possession. Their course, however, was condemned by citizens generally, and on the 3d of June some warrants were taken out, and Sheriff Sevier, accompanied by some deputies, went to make the arrests. C. A. Sherman, William Mc- Donald, alias "Billy the Rake," and a man by the name of Baker, were all that could be found. They were taken in custody by the Sheriff", and carried before Justice Hansell, of Eureka, who held them to bail in the sum of 13,000 each, on a charge of murder. Sherman and McDonald gave bail, and Baker was committed to jail, where he still remains.
——Sacramento Daily Union, Volume 15, Number 2260, 24 June 1858

[also repeated almost verbatim in a history: Indian wars of the Northwest: A California sketch, CHAPTER XV, By A.J. Bledsoe.]

From: Loud: Ethnogeography and Archaeology of the Wiyot Territory 327. 1918
University of California Publications in Am. Arch. and Ethn. [Vol. 14] pp 327, 328:

In May, 1858, a theft occurred on Eel river which was more serious in its consequences to the Indians. Robertson Jack, a bad Indian, stole a Mr. Kady's gun, hiding it and not advising even his relatives that he had it. Kady was very angry about his loss for two or three days. Then, when one day Jack brought home ten rabbits, his uncle suspected, watched him, and discovered the hiding place. Dandy Bill and his uncle started to take the gun back to its owner, but, fearing trouble, left it with Dungan. Kady was satisfied when he got hisgun, but certain other white men desired to punish the Indians and attacked the village, site Ax, at daybreak one morning, killing Dandy Bill's uncle, the uncle's wife, and a baby, and wounding another woman so that she died later. Dandy Bill's father buried his brother at site 104, while Dandy Bill went to Fort Humboldt and carried legal papers back and forth between the judge and the sheriff, who subsequently arrested three white men, C. A. Sherman, William McDonald, and a man named Baker.

Daily Alta California, Volume 10, Number 177, 29 June 1858:
Three of the party implicated in the murder of some Indiana on Eel River have been indicted for the crime.

[Note: none of these accounts mention James Grush. Only the following from the Humboldt Times does.]

From Van Kirk, Susie, "Fort Humboldt Conflict Period" [items from the Humboldt Times]:
(Humboldt Editor Austin Wiley, 23 Jan. 1858 to 16 June 1860)

HT (19 June 1858) Don't Like It—Some men in the lower end of the county are very indignant at our article last week, concerning the Indian difficulty on Eel river and the character of the men who did the shooting. They think we did wrong in giving the names of some of the parties. All we regret is that we did not have all their names, so we could hold them up to the public as they deserve. Two men named Wideman and Grush, we have since learned, were leaders in this cowardly attack. They are said to be bad men and continually creating trouble with the Indians….

p.s. Since the above was in type, we learn that Sherman has been surrendered by his bondsman to the Sheriff and is now in jail, awaiting the action of the Grand Jury.

HT (26 June 1858) Grand Jury Report—indictments against Sherman, McDonald, Baker, Wideman and Grush for murder.

HT (26 June 1858) Killing Indians—In an article in our issue of the 12th inst., we mentioned the circumstances of the killing of some Indians on Eel River, among whom were a squaw and child. We condemned the shooting and animadverted in pretty strong terms on a certain class of men in this county known as "squaw men." Three of the party charged with the killing of these Indians are now waiting their trial on an indictment for murder, which prevents us from following this particular subject any further or from expressing any opinion, or making any remarks calculated to effect public sentiment in regard to the guilt or innocents of the men.
… Our mode of warfare with Indians is to pay them off in their own coin. If they murder a white man without cause, kill then Indians for it. Let them understand that we will be governed by the same mode of revenge as themselves, and depredations will then cease. On the other hand, Indians should have reciprocal protection by the whites. We do not grant that any men is entitled to the privilege of misusing or abusing Indians, or their squaws.

Appendix L

The Family of Alexander James Grush
(Mayor of Naperville, Illinois)

By Byron E. Grush, Jr.
Delavan, Wisconsin, December, 2011

My grandfather, Alexander James Grush, was born July 14, 1869 in Ogle County, Illinois, near Polo in the township of Pine Creek. His father and mother, John B. Grush and Mary Jane (Tennis) Grush, had a farm there, near the farm of John's father (Alex's grandfather), Isaac Grush. Isaac had been born in Lancaster County, Pennsylvania in 1802 and moved to Huntington County, Pennsylvania where he married Catherine Burns and raised the first eight of his eleven children.

Isaac moved his family to Illinois in 1845 or 1846 to take advantage of the rich farmland being offered for sale by the Illinois Central Railroad. The price of land was $1.50 per acre and Isaac bought 160 acres. He had come all the way by water, on the Ohio and Mississippi Rivers by raft or flatboat. My Great Grandfather, John B. Grush, was one of the eight children he brought to settle in Ogle County, Illinois, near Polo.

John Grush was born October 21, 1827, in Shirleysburg Township, Huntingdon County, Pennsylvania. The region was mountainous, broken up by ridges and valleys and drained by the Juniata River. The river flats provided rich soil for farming and the abundance of iron ore and other minerals presented an opportunity for mining. There was a section called German Valley that attracted many of that ancestry from Lancaster County in the eastern part of the state, where John's father, Isaac was born.

John's farm in Illinois was section 17, across the road from his father's on section 19, in the Pine Creek Township of Ogle County, Illinois. The land must have seemed flat after Pennsylvania and would have needed breaking in by plow. In May of 1861, John married Mary Jane Tennis. She was born on December 8, 1835, in Indiana, to William (b. 1804 in PA) and Delila (b. 1806 in VA) Tennis. They were married in Ogle County. A daughter, Ida May, was born on June 22, 1861. In March of 1866, a second daughter, Hattie Emma born. Grandfather Alexander was born July 14, 1869.

Pine Creek Township was about 120 miles from Chicago where supplies were bought once a year as it was a journey of several days. Eventually, the Grushes began taking local meat products to Chicago to sell. Grandfather Alexander must have been involved in this enterprise as it fits nicely into his later career running a meat market in Naperville. Alexander married Ida Birdellen Toms from neighboring Mt. Morris village on November 9, 1893. She was born in 1874 to Charles Toms and Mary Elizabeth (Wolz) Toms. Ida Birdellen Toms was a descendant of Major John George Adam Wolz who fought in the American Revolutionary War. In later years she was a member of the Daughters of the American Revolution.

Alex and "Birdie" may have moved into town in Polo, but I have been unable to document this. A first child, Vernon Charles Grush came along on January 1, 1896 and in 1900, a daughter, Shirley was born. The family then moved to Naperville, Illinois in 1907. Alexander, along with a Mr. Faulhaber, opened a meat market and butcher shop downtown. My father, Byron E. Grush, Sr., was born in their apartment upstairs from the shop.

There was a magnitude of commerce between the farmers of the prairie and the denizens of Chicago, aided by the establishment of venues for the transportation of goods. The Old Plank Road eventually fell to defects in engineering, as the boards that had been laid down warped, slipped and decayed, and so the railroad took over the task of delivering goods from the team driven wagons. The Grushes, growing grain and raising livestock, certainly traveled this path. Alexander Grush would have been familiar with the potential of the new town of Naperville and chose to bring his family there around 1907.

As I write this, Naperville's population is 142,075. In 1907 it was more like 2,000. Some of the dirt roads and wooden sidewalks had been replaced by paving but it was not until 1910 that downtown got its red brick pavement. There was a brewery, a cheese factory, a fly-net manufacturer (fly-nets draped across horses to ward off insects), the Naper Academy and the North western College (later called North Central College). Grush and Faulhaber's Meat Market was at 27 West Jefferson Street. A meat market has operated at that location until very recently.

Alex was a friendly proprietor and accepted payment from his customers in whatever form they presented. He saved the coins from the various countries they paid with and I was lucky enough to inherit this collection of German, Swiss and other European money. When the circus came to town, however, he refused to sell the pigs' and calves' legs requested by sideshow operators because, as my grandmother told the story, he knew they would try to defraud the public by attaching the dead animals' legs to members of their "freak show."

Grandfather was a crusty entrepreneur, but often his investments went wrong. In the 1920s he bought land in California from a developer who, unfortunately, didn't own the land he was selling. Alex and many other unwary investors were summarily bilked of their money. He was a success in the gasoline business, though, opening Naperville's first filling station in 1922. It was located on north Washington Street where later Moser Lumber Company built a store and where the Naperville Children's Museum stands today. Byron, Sr., joined Alex in the business and by 1934, had created the Grush Oil Company, selling heating oil in conjunction with his father. Byron worked hard, installing oil burners for free to convert old coal furnaces to the newer fuel.

The first house Alex and his family lived in in Naperville was on Main Street, south of the downtown. They later moved to 151 N. Wright Street, across from the old Kroehler mansion which later became a seminary. He had been active in local politics, served as a commissioner and had finished out the term of the city's then Mayor Bowman in 1921, so it was natural for him to run for mayor again in 1931. He was elected to a four year term during the country's worst depression, and that first year saw the City of Naperville's Centennial.

He was an active participant in the planning and running of events for the centennial celebration. My grandmother remembered stuffing invitations and brass medallions into envelops. Silk American flags were given out. It is said that the parade on the second day of the celebration was five miles long and took two hours to pass any one point along the route. A recreational park was dedicated near the old stone quarries and the "double quarry" was purchased to be turned into a swimming beach--- a large and unique place lined with flag stone with a sandy area which has attracted people to Naperville since its inception. I remember going there to swim as a child, waiting in line to be admitted to the locker room and pointing out proudly to my friends the brass commemorative plaque with the name, Major Alexander J. Grush on it. "That's my grandfather," I would announce.

During the depression, Mayor Grush helped organize soup kitchens in town. There was a Relief Society formed by local women to try to feed the needy but their efforts needed enhancing. The mayor and the City Council authorized the creation of a soup kitchen and a group of business men called the Knife and Fork Club helped to fund it. Genevieve Towsley, in one of her articles interviewed the man who did the cooking:

"We set up 20-foot tables along the west side of the light plant.... Every day either Mayor Alexander Grush of Commissioner George Keller would bring me soup bones which they collected from the butchers.

"There were days when we fed over a hundred. I went to work at 7 a.m. and often didn't quit before 10 p.m. because we had hobos coming in during the evening and wanting a meal. They'd stay all night in the jail and eat breakfast (soup) before moving on."

Vernon Grush, who we called "Uncle Boney," fought in World War I. I believe he was in France around the time of the Armistice. My father, 12 years the younger, wrote him a touching letter which still exists in which he stated how much he wished the war would end. Vernon married Madelyn Coombs and they lived in neighboring Downers Grove. Their daughters, Sue, Rosemary and Jane, were older than me by two decades and seemed more like aunts than cousins. Still I enjoyed our visits to Uncle Boney's house.

My Aunt Shirley had married a man named Homer Boelter and moved to California. I never met her. I was closer, I guess, to my aunt and uncle on my mother's side, Aunt Ellen and Uncle Lester Broeker. Lester Broeker and my father were the town cut ups in their youth. There are stories of the two of them racing their cars through town and driving on the sidewalks. I don't know if this is true or not, but I always enjoyed how the stories would be cut off abruptly when we children were present. Lester's father, Carl Broeker had bought the Williard Scott dry goods store in Naperville in 1905. Lester joined the firm in 1929 and Broeker's was the biggest and best department store in the county for years to come.

Lester and my father met and married two Swedish sisters from Superior, Wisconsin, who had teaching jobs in the Naperville schools. My mother was Olga Olson and my aunt was Ellen Olson, the daughters of John and Sophia Johanna (Swenson) Olson, Swedish immigrants who settled in Northern Wisconsin. There were four brothers and two sisters in the family… but that's another story.

Alexander Grush died on April 1, 1945. I was 1 ½ years old so I don't remember him except from stories and the very few photographs that exist. My favorite photo of him is the one where he is wearing a full Indian headdress. I did spend many of my childhood moments at my grandmother's house, at lunch time or after school. I remember she had a huge potted fern in her dining room whose leaves she warned me never to touch or the plant would shrivel up and die. She had some peculiar ideas, I thought. We spent hours once arguing over whether God had made Eve from Adam's rib, or Adam from Eve's rib. She argued for the latter. Alex was a Mason and Birdie was in the Eastern Star. She had also been in an amateur theater group that put on mistral shows, or so I've been told.

I think now about all these people that are gone and realize how little I actually know about their lives. What was it like to sail from your native country across the ocean to an unfamiliar land peopled with Indians and men about to engage in revolution? To travel by raft on unfriendly rivers in order to carve out a living from difficult terrain with oxen and plow? And Alex, who I think of as much a pioneer as his father and grandfather before him, perhaps contributing to the maturation of a small town, being part of the fabric of its personality. To quote Willa Cather, "O Pioneers!"

Appendix M
U.S. Army Base Hospital No. 13, Limoges, France

Base Hospital No.13 was organized in July 1916, at the Presbyterian Hospital (might be what is known as the famous Presbyterian St. Lukes today?), Chicago, Ill. On January 11, 1918, the unit was mobilized in Chicago, and proceeded January 19, 1918, to Fort Mc Pherson, Ga., for training and equipment. The organization left Fort McPherson May 1, 1918, for Camp Merrit, N. J., and embarked May 19, on the Saturnia for Europe. It arrived in Le Havre, France, May 31, 1918, and proceeded on June 8 to its permanent station at Limoges, Department of Haute Vienne, base section No. 2. It arrived at Limoges June 10, and formed a part of what was to be the hospital center there.

The unit occupied 52 wooden buildings, constructed by the engineers, located in a park near the center of the city. The normal capacity of the hospital was 1500 beds, but in October and November, 1918, it was expanded to 2300 beds. The first patients arrived July 19, 1918; the total number cared for was 6267, of which 3,648 were surgical and 2,619 medical cases, with 965 operations. The largest number of patients in hospital was 2,323 sick and wounded on November 13,1918.

Appendix N, Charles Berger:

Census for Pine Creek Township, 1880, shows Charles Berger living with John B. Grush
[Note: Anne Eshelman, step daughter and Cora Shafer, adopted daughter]

Charles B. Berger, a resident of the township of Pine Creek, is the son of William W. and Annie (Lee) Berger. The former a native of Pennsylvania and was born Jan. 6, 1835; the latter was the son of Samuel and Hannah (Barnes) Berger, who were also born in the Keystone State. They came to Illinois about 1849 and located in Lee County, where the mother died. The father of William Berger married Roxey Webster, who was born in the State of New York. They were both living in Polo. William W. Berger was married Sept. 4, 1862, at Milton, Rock County, Wis., and returned with his wife to Ogle County, where they passed the ensuing winter.

In the spring of the next year Mr. Berger went to Pike's Peak with a company, and started from there for New Mexico, and was killed by the marauding Indians on the plains. The bereaved wife returned to Wisconsin, where her son was born in Janesville, Rock County, Aug. 8, 1863. She was still living there when she was married to Mr. John Grush, of Pine Creek Township, of whom a sketch will be found elsewhere in this book. Charles B. Berger came to Ogle County with his step-father and remained on the farm assisting him in the summer, and in the winter attending school at Polo. Later, he attended the college at Mt. Morris, where he was a student until within a few weeks of graduation, when he went to Janesville, to enter upon the duties of a clerk in the store of his uncle,

Samuel Holdridge, who was a prominent merchant of that place. Previous to going there he had been for a time in Dakota. In the spring of 1882 he came back to Illinois, and accepted a situation in the clothing store ofa business firm at Polo, where here remained until February, 1883. He went then to Ipswich, D. T., and, in company with T. J. Winters, managed the Star Restaurant. After doing business there for the space of a year, he returned to Illinois. He engaged in the capacity of a sewing-machine agent, in the interest of D. R. Rogers, of Polo. Here remained in his employ until the fall of 1885, when he entered the employ of a merchant in Polo, where he is at present operating. He is a young man of excellent character, and a popular and efficient salesman.

——Portrait and Biographical Album of Ogle County, Illinois

Appendix O
The Olson Family and Olga Grush trip to Sweden, 1970:

Fred, Father John Olson, Ellen, Mother Sophia holding Olga, and Richard

Mrs. Byron (Olga) Grush fulfilled a longtime dream last month--visiting Sweden, the homeland of her parents. To prepare for her trip, she began to study Swedish three years ago, and to correspond with a cousin in the village of Eksharad, in the province of Varmland (warm land).

Deciding to visit other Scandinavian countries, she flew to Paris the middle of May; and, after a day there, to Copenhagen. Tours of that city and a three-day tour of the Danish countryside were an enjoyable prelude to her stay in Sweden, although she found the weather cold and damp.

In Stockholm, a severe sore throat prompted her to ask for medical help. In that country of socialized medicine she was advised to telephone a doctor, to whom she was referred. This she did. The physician, after hearing her description of her symptons, diagnosed her problem as a "strep throat", and told her what "apotek" (drug store) to patronize, in order to get the medicine which he would prescribe, and in order to pay his bill. Her bill for his services and the medicine was $3!

The discomfort of her throat did not prevent her from sightseeing in Stockholm or going to Eksharad, where she was a guest of her cousin Kerstin Jansson, who operates a dairy farm on a lake. What joy it was to meet the handsome, blonde many cousins-50 of them-in that village and its vicinity! There were parties and smorgasbord feasts every day.

Olga gave a party in the inn for all of them, where they had a wonderful time dancing and singing together.

'Twas a truly emotional experience to visit the ancient homes of her father and her mother. The Olsson house, where her father lived, is centuries old, with mammoth fireplaces in each of its rooms, including eight bedrooms. It has been inherited by the eldest son of each generation. Her mother's home is being restored for its historical value, and still has in it the quaint furnishings that her mother knew. On the property is a building with a sod roof. The present owners, seeing Olga's rapture with their home, gave her a rare wooden memento, carved by her great-great grandfather in 1767.

"It is a strange-looking object," declares Olga, "resembling a carpenter's plane. Actually it is a forerunner of a mangle. Housewives wrapped their handwoven linens around it to iron them. It was a tradition for each young man to carve one of these for his sweetheart. If she accepted it, when he proffered it to her, it indicated her consent to marry him. If she refused, he must seek another prospect and carve another ironing device to offer her. These are now quite scarce and valuable antiques."

Olga's throat worsened at her cousin's home, and she developed bronchitis and laryngitis. Once again she consulted a physician by phone, following the previous procedure to obtain treatment. When her problem persisted, even after she reached Oslo, Norway, she decided to seek help once again, before going on a fjord trip. There, too, the physician only spoke to her on the phone, assuring her that it was warm in Norway, and that she would soon be free of her chest problem. On the fjord trip, she met a young woman from Yugoslavia who had a supply of drugs with her, and who gave her some sulpha pills. Within a day or two she was feeling fit and happy not to have to partronize a system of socialized medicine again!

In a hotel lobby in Oslo, she met—quite by coincidence—her friend Gladys Gerber from Naperville! Gladys and her sister were doing the same in Norway as Olga did in Sweden—visiting their parents' childhood home. Olga joined them on a tour of Oslo before her fjord trip.

Two days in London rounded out her trip before she flew home. Met at O'Hare field by Byron, she was not prepared to find all her children and their families awaiting her at home. Jim, with his wife and two little girls, had come from Boston. (He is studying at Boston University for his Ph.D., but will play with the Boston Symphony orchestra this summer at Tanglewood.) Mary Ellen, who attends Fort Wright College in Spokane, Washington, had returned home, and also there were Byron Jr., his wife, Margo, and their little girl—from Highland Park. It was a heart-warming homecoming at the end of a dream trip.

I'll be with you next week.

Genevieve Towsley

Appendix P

Samuel Fuller (born c.1580/1 – died in Plymouth between August 9 and September 26, 1633) He was a passenger on the historic 1620 voyage of the Pilgrim ship Mayflower and became a respected church deacon and the physician for Plymouth Colony.
——http://en.wikipedia.org/wiki/Samuel_Fuller_(Pilgrim)

1. Samuel Fuller (born c.1580/1 – died in Plymouth between August 9 and September 26, 1633)
+ Bridget Lee in Leiden on May 27, 1617. She died May 2, 1667 - she married Samuel Fuller on May 12, 1617 [wife #3]
2. Rev. Samuel Fuller born about 1629. Samuel died on August 17, 1695. (2nd child)
+ Elizabeth (Nicholas) Bowen - married between April 11, 1663, and May 2, 1667, and had six children
3. Dr. Isaac Fuller b poss 1674, d. c 1722
+ Mary Pratt sep 1, 1709 - 9 children
4. Lt. Isaac Fuller b 12-15-1738, d 8-22-1804 (1st child)
+ Mary Alden b Aug 5, 1745 (Plymouth?), d Sept 9 1818 (father Daniel Alden, mother Abigail Shaw- 5th gen of John Alden)
5. Lemuel Fuller b. May 12, 1768, d Feb 23, 1796 (2nd of 8 children)
+ Fanny Hriggs b Oct 17, 1778, d Feb 14, 1831
6. William Nelson Fuller b Apr 22, 1815, d Nov 23, 1887
+ Caroline Lorina married Nov 29, 1843, d Jan 22, 1879
7. Fanny Briggs Fuller b. Mar 22, 1852, d Oct 8, 1920
+ Chadwick Gale b. Apr 13, 1847, d Apr 9, 1926
8. Gertie (Gertrude) Fannie Gale b Jun 25, 1899, d Sept 24, 1954
+ Charles Cleveland Pierson b. July 2, 1884, d Mar 10, 1973- married May 10, 1911
9- Albert Chadwick Pierson
Beatrice Jane Pierson
Fanny Gale Pierson

Appendix Q
Wedding of Ellen Olson to Lester Broeker:

Left to right: Olga, Ellen, and Lily Olson about 1914

Wedding Is Read Today

Miss Ellen Olson Bride of Naperville Man; Leave Today on Trip

At 2:30 o'clock this afternoon the marriage of Miss Ellen Willene Olson to Lester Lawrence Broeker of Naperville, Ill., was solemnized at a beautiful informal ceremony at the home of the bride's parents Mr. and Mrs. John Olson, 170 Twenty-eighth street. The Rev Samuel Hogander, pastor of First Covenant church, performed the ceremony in the presence of the immediate families and intimate friends of the bride and groom.

The living room was effectively decorated with palms banked with tall baskets of white peonies and plumosi ferns. The tall lighted candles in candelabra added to the bridal atmosphere. Preceding the ceremony Miss Dorothy Kuhlmer sang "O Promise Me" and "I Love You Truly," and while Miss Eva Downs played the "Bridal Chorus" from "Lohengrin" the bridal party descended the open stairway leading to the improvised altar where the vows were exchanged.

Bride Wears Blue.

The bride, who was given in marriage by her father, was lovely in a floor length dress of old lace fashioned on princess lines with a short train. She wore matching footwear and a wreath of white sweet peas in her hair. Her arm bouquet was white Killarney roses, white sweet peas and gypsophila, tied with a white lace bow. Her only jewelry was a baguette wrist watch, a gift of the groom.

Miss Olga Olson, a sister of the bride, was bridesmaid, wearing a floor length dress of pink organza with a blue velvet bow at the neck. She wore matching footwear and a wreath of blue forget-me-nots, and carried an arm bouquet of Briar Cliff roses and butterfly sweet peas tied with a pale pink bow. The bridegroom was attended by Byron E. Grush, son of Mayor and Mrs. A. Grush of Naperville.

Mrs. Olson, the bride's mother, was dressed in brown and beige print with matching accessories, and wore a similar corsage of Talisman roses and orchid sweet peas. Mrs. Carl Broeker of Naperville, mother of the bridegroom, had a black and white ensemble with white accessories, and a shoulder corsage of pink and white sweet peas.

The dining room was decorated with tall white candles and bouquets of pink sweet peas, pink larkspur and gypsophila in silver bowls for the wedding reception which followed the ceremony. The wedding cake, surrounded by smilax, formed the centerpiece for the bridal table.

Out-of-Town Guests.

Among the 50 guests who were present were the following from out of town: Mr. and Mrs. Carl Broeker, Misses Ruth and Elaine Broeker, and Byron E. Grush, all of Naperville, Ill.; Mrs. Rena Cummings, Seattle, Wash., and Mr. and Mrs. William Boyer, Cloquet, Minn. Besides the immediate family of the bride, Superior guests included Mr. and Mrs. E. T. Safford, Mr. and Mrs. Harry C. Kelly, Mr. and Mrs. R. Adamson, Mrs. Alice Penfound, Mrs. N. O. Fjerstad, Miss Mona Penfound and Miss Florence Henderson. Misses Alice and Dorothy Safford assisted during the reception.

Immediately after the reception the bride and groom will leave on an extended wedding trip through Canada and the New England states, visiting en route in Montreal, Quebec, Albany, New York and Boston before returning to Chicago. The bride is wearing a going-away costume of brown and white net, with matching accessories and shoulder corsage of pink roses.

After August 1 they will be at home at 730 East Chicago avenue, Naperville, Ill.

Appendix R, Grush Reunions:

GRUSH FAMILY HAS INITIAL REUNION

Forty-three Gather at "The Pines" Sunday; Plan to Hold Gathering Annually

Forty-three descendants of Isaac and Catherine Burns Grush gathered at "The Pines" State Park Sunday for a reunion. A scramble dinner at noon was followed by a most enjoyable social time.

The decision to hold the reunion annually was reached at the business session when officers were elected. Those present included residents of Chicago, Batavia, LaGrange, Downers Grove, Freeport, Lanark, Mount Morris and Polo.

Following are the officers elected: president, Dr. B. A. Arnold, Freeport; vice-presidents, Alex Grush of Naperville and Gertrude Grush of Mt. Morris; secretary and treasurer, E. R. Wagner, Chicago, corresponding secretaries, Kathryn Parks, Polo, and Ina Dunn, Freeport; historian, Byron Grush, Naperville; program committee, Mrs. J. C. Lampin, Polo, Mrs. Hattie Horner, Lanark, Gladys Jones, Mt. Morris.

Appendix S, More about Mayor Alex Grush:

During the early 1930s a newspaper was published in Naperville, Illinois named *Naperville Events*. The editor, Magnus Arnold, was a bit of a muckraker and took the city council and the mayor to task often. He had a cartoonist named Ed Lueben who drew caricatures like these from 1931. Reprinted by the Naperville Sun:

Naperville's "Whispering Council," as depicted by Ed Lueben, bears remarkable likeness to the 1931 city council. Oldtimers will easily identify them (left to right) as John Bentz, Charles Wellner, Mayor Alex Grush, George Keller, and Joe Yender.

From "Skylines" by Genevieve Towsley, Naperville Sun, Jan 20, 1982:

...The spring of 1931 was a good time It was also a bad time It was the time that Naperville celebrated its centennial with a mammoth parade and an elaborate pageant. The event was commemorated by the acquisition of Centennial Park, site of our Centennial Beach. It was the time when the city was in the grip of the Depression. Building had ceased. Unemployment was on the rise. Wages and prices had plummeted. The spring of 1931 also marked the emergence of a monthly news magazine on the Naperville scene. It was "Naperville Events." edited and published by Magnus Arnold and Son. "Devoted to the best interests of our citizens and our community." it measured 6V x 10" and was mailed free of charge to every household bearing a Naperville address....

New faces joined the City Council the same month that "Naperville Events" first arrived in the city's mail boxes. Alex Grush was elected mayor. Councilmen were Charles Wellner, John Bentz, Joseph Yender, and George Keller. Arnold was present when they were inducted in- to office, and he attended all the council meetings thereafter —until he became disgusted with the councilmen's practice of huddling together and whispering. He named them the "Whispering Council" and regularly berated them for their actions or the lack of them....

In the same magazine Arnold called attention to the fact that Grush and Co., the mayor's oil company, had submitted 15 bills to the city during the four months since the mayor took office. The following month he printed the Illinois Statute on the subject of a city official selling supplies to the city. Such an act should be "punished by a fine of not less than $100 or more than $500, and shall be ground for removal from office."

[Nothing came of it. Grush and Company stopped selling the city gas and oil. Arnold's publication ceased.]

From "A SMALL TOWN WEATHERS THE DEPRESSION Naperville, Illinois, 1929-39" by Doris Wood, 1972:

…During the depression years, Naperville had three mayors, Bill Thompson, Alexander Grush and Jim Nichols. Thompson lost to Grush in the 1931 municipal election with 2, 537 votes cast. Grush's commissioners were George Keller, John Bentz, Charles V. VJellner and Joseph Yender Jr., and his pet projects were the beach and the soup kitchen.

"We set up four twenty-foot tables along the west side of the city light plant," Ulrich recalled. "The American Legion loaned us dishes and silver and bought six big kettles to cook the soup in. Every day, either Mayor Alex Grush or Commissioner George Keller would bring me soup bones which they had collected from the butchers."

EAST END

MEAT MARKET

Refitted, Freshened and Cleansed invites your patronage and will strive to merit it by selling the Choicest

FRESH AND

SALTED MEATS

At Reasonable Rates   Please Call and See Us

N B –Highest Prices Paid for Veals and Hides

GRUSH & ELIOTT,

POLO, ILLINOIS,

Ogle County Press, published in Polo, Illinois on Saturday, February 10th, 1894
[precursor to Grush and Faulhaber Meat Market in Naperville?]

Addendum (No Relations):

In researching the name Grush I came across many Grushes who were not related to my line, at least as far as I could determine. I profile some of them here because, like the unrelated Grosh lines, I find them interesting, and their stories are worth telling. Who knows, if you go back far enough, perhaps there are some links to our lineage.

S. W. Grush

A map of Nevada City, California in 1856 published by J. E. Hamlin, Bookseller presents a "bird's eye view" of the city surrounded by 34 vignettes of buildings. Among these is S.W. Grush, Pacific Restaurant. Grush and a man named Parker owned the U. S. Hotel, also called the Monument Hotel there. It burned and was rebuilt at least once, possibly more (*Brides of the gold rush, 1851-1859* - David A. Comstock – 1987, Page 288: "We have as yet received no reliable accounts of lives lost S. W. Grush, of the Monumental Hotel . . . was also a heavy loser in the fire of July [1856]. Mr. Grush informs us that this is the fourth time he has been ruined by the elements…") and (Marysville Daily Appeal, Volume I, Number 131, 22 June 1860: "The losses by the fire on Tuesday were not heavy… Grush & Parker, proprietors of the U. S. Hotel lose…"). The California State Census of 1852 show him as born in 1820 in Maine. I found in *The Argonauts of California: Being the Reminiscences of Scenes and Incidents that Occurred in California in Early Mining Days*, - *Voyages to the Pacific coast* Fords, Howard & Hulbert, 1890 (Google eBook), that S. W. Grush arrived in California on the Ship Drummond from Boston on February 1, 1849(?).

Also from Nevada Journal, Volume 3, Number 49, 31 March 1854: "Woodpecker Ravine —Last week, Messrs. Bicknell, Grush & Co., three men, took out 52 ounces, from their claims, being near three ounces a day to the hand." Woodpecker Ravine is in Nevada County.

UNITED STATES HOTEL

[Broad Street, near Pine

We take pleasure in informing the public that we are now prepared to accommodate travellers in as comfortable a style as any Hotel in the mountains. It will be our constant aim to render our house as pleasant a retreat as can be found anywhere.

Prices are moderate and as fair an equivalent will be returned for cash received as the times will allow.

Those of our friends who formerly favored us with their patronage at the Monumental are assured that they will find the same comforts in our new establishment as were found in the old.

Meals........Fifty Cents.
Lodgings 50 and 75 cents.
GRUSH & PARKER, Proprietors,
Nevada, Sept 3d,1858.

The Nevada journal. October 05, 1860

From Sacramento Daily Union, Monday, January 2, 1865, Page 6:
DEATHS September 6-Samuel W. GRUSH, Massachusetts, 45 years

Capt. John Grush
From: A Partial List of Those Who Are Buried at Old Burial Hill, Marblehead, Massachusetts—
Capt. John Grush, a.54y., 2 mos., 9 Jan.1787. John Grush m. Hannah Collyer, 6 Dec. 1757.

The Bellona [Velona] was a Massachusetts Privateer Brigantine [Brig] commissioned 29 April 1777 under Commander Thomas Stevens of Marblehead, Massachusetts. She was listed as being armed with fourteen guns and as having a crew of ninety men. Her Owners were (1) James Mugford et al of Marblehead, Massachusetts; (2) Samuel White of Boston, Massachusetts and John Grush of Marblehead, Massachusetts. Bellona was at sea in the late summer. Bellona (under Stevens) was mentioned in the Boston Gazette of 22 September 1777.2 At least two prizes were captured. Bellona was re-commissioned on 1 January 1778 under Commander Nicholas Ogelbe of Marblehead. She was listed as having a battery of fourteen guns and a crew of seventy-five men. Her $5000 Continental bond and her £500 Massachusetts bond were executed by Ogelbe, and by Major Samuel White of Boston, Massachusetts and John Grush of Marblehead. White and Grush are listed as Bellona's owners.

——awiatsea.com

The Conestoga Wagon Wagon Makers of Lancaster County
In colonial days it was almost essential for a farmer to have working knowledge of a blacksmith, and a blacksmith to be able to sustain his family by farming. In fact in Lancaster County where the Conestoga wagons were produced, there is a List of Blacksmiths in the Townships of Lancaster County from 1729 to 1840 which lists approximately fifteen hundred blacksmiths. Wagon Makers, Wheelwrights, Blacksmith from the Wagoners Tax Assessment Records of Lancaster County for Townships of the Conestoga Valley Area are listed below. The dates given are the first time the person appeared on the list:
Earl Township
Grush, Stopher 1780   Blacksmith
      ——Source: Research and Text by Bryan Wright;
      http://www.colonialsense.com/Society-
      Lifestyle/Signs_of_the_Times/Conestoga_Wagon/Wagon_Makers.php

[it is possible that the given name, Stopher, has been shortened from Christopher…or maybe not.]

Crew of USS Constitution, 1812
Crew of Old Ironsides who sailed her early 19th Century
From "Black Notebook #46", Marblehead Historical Commission, historic@marblehead.org

Listed there is Grush, Robert Wooldridge.
He also appears in "Salem, Mass. Crew Lists Index: 1799-1879" on the Iris (Schooner) as a 21-year-old in 12/09/1809. This same list shows a Joseph Grush, Position Cook, on three ships, Martha (Brig) age 16 on 05/02/1809, Fame (Schooner) age 17 on 08/24/1810, and Indus (Ship) age 22 on 7/24/1815. Joseph sailed to the West Indies, Mantanzas, the South Seas & China.
      ——http://library.mysticseaport.org/initiative/SalemSelect.cfm

Job Henry Grush
Birth: abt 1826. Residence: 1866 - San Francisco, California, United States. California, Voter Registers, 1866-1898 1930s

From Boston Around Cape Horn to Valparaiso, 1849-50:

Since the writer of the letter states that her ship, the brig Colorado, had made the run from Boston to St. Catherine's (an island off the coast of Brazil, some distance southwest of Rio de Janeiro) in sixty-one days, and since the Colorado apparently lay at St. Catherine's for several days, resuming her voyage on 2nd January 1850, the brig must have sailed from Boston about the latter part of October 1849.

Brig COLORADO - Harbor of Valparaiso - March 31 1850

Mr. I. E. Sanborn
Dear Sir,
...Jan. 28th made Cape Horn. Jan. 30th commenced with light winds from S E (our true course was west). At 10am wind S W increasing to a gale. At 4pm Coast of Terra del Fuego on our lea 15 miles distant...
The Passengers looked on in Silence while the Capt. and Mate consulted maps and charts. It was a long and sleepless night for us all. At daylight we had passed the cape, how near we could not exactly tell but we where [sic] close in to land, the wind favored us 2 points we tacked ship and stood out to sea, thankfull [sic] enough for plenty of sea room. When we where [sic] a hundred miles or so from land, we lay too [sic] and when the gale was over cleared up the wreck. We where [sic] five weeks beating about with gale after gale-- what we gained one day we lost the next by laying too. [sic] February 26th Lattitude [sic] 53° 43 South Longitude 77° 30, Capt. Baker united in Marriage Mr. Job Henry Grush of Roxbury and Miss Mary Jane Stinchfield. The parties were not acquainted before coming on board. The Capt. published them at Morning Prayers. Excitement and curiosity privailed [sic] for the intended wedding was known to but few. Jokes passed. Love, Courtship and Marriage was talked of. The morning was spent in moving beds, boxes trunks, and preparing a room for the Bride. At 4 O'Clock pm the bride and groom made the appearance neatly dressed. Mr. Woods of Boston and myself had the honor of standing up with them. The gong was rung. The gentlemen Passengers came out on this Occasion in fancy costume, different nations fashions trades Shapes and Colours where [sic] represented--most all wore enormous paper collars, Small men where [sic] stuffed to twice there [sic] usual size. Swords, Pistols, Eppiletts [sic] Guns, rings, eyeglasses, Tartan plaids and Policemen with badges where [sic] all there, while the representative from Sweet Irelande [sic] keept [sic] the door with a Shelalah [sic] in his hand. Perfect order was maintained while the marriage ceremony was read and prayer offered, then came kisses and congratulations for the Bride and nine hearty cheers for the groom. An extra supper was provided. At midnight they where [sic] serenaded by the Owl Club of which Mr. Grush was a member--thus ended our Cape Horn wedding--a time that will long be remembered by us all--we all thought that such an important event would bring us a fair wind. It came a few days after and we had a good run to this port...
I am you friend -- Ellen M. Knights

——"The Forty-Niners"
New England Historical Genealogical Register - vol. 90 - pp. 32-41 - Jan. 1936
https://www.theshipslist.com/ships/passengerlists/Forty-Niners.shtml

Bibliography

Album of Ogle Co., IL, Chapman Bros., Chicago, IL Portrait and Biographical, 1886, page 477

Baer, Willis N., The Genealogy of Henry Baer, 1955

Bare, D. M., Looking Eighty Years Backward And A History of Roaring Spring

Bledsoe, A.J. Indian wars of the Northwest: A California sketch, CHAPTER XV

Bomberber, William Edward, History of the Isaac Grush Family

Carlock, Marion Pomeroy. History of the Carlock Family and Adventures of Pioneer Americans Including the Kimbrough, Goodpasture, Hoyl, Fite, Fancher, Lee, Wells, Judy, Tracy, Settles, Gaddis, Rowell, Moore, Cornelison, Harrold, Brown and Other Connecting Families. (Los Angeles [California]: M.P. Carlock, 1929) CD-ROM.

Clarke. The Biographical record of Ogle County, Illinois. S.J. Clarke Publishing Company.

Customs & Practices of the Moravian Church, Crews & Starbuck, 2003."

Eby, Ezra E., The History of the Eby Family 1889 p. 112

Egle. Egle's History of Huntingdon County, 1883.

Kett, H.F. The history of Ogle County, Illinois. Kett, H.F. & Co. Chicago

Kingery, Solomon. Overland Letters. Western Americana Collection, Beinecke Rare Book and Manuscript Library, Yale University. from typed transcription

Loud: Ethnogeography and Archaeology of the Wiyot Territory 327. 1918 University of California

Publications in Am. Arch. and Ethn. [Vol. 14] pp 327, 328:

McLung, Zara. Travals Across the Plains in 1852. Chambers and Knapp, St. Louis, MO. 1854

Miller, Joaquin. Joaquin Miller's Romantic Life Amongst the Red Indians: An Autobiography. Saxon & Company, 1890.

Miller, Joaquin. Life Amongst the Modocs: Unwritten History. American Publishing Company, Hartford, Conn. 1874.

Mount Morris: past and present: an illustrated history of the township and the village of Mount Morris, Ogle County, Illinois, in their various stages of development, together with a local biographical directory (Google eBook)

Ogle County Atlas, Everts, Baskin & Stewart, 1872

Pennsylvania Historical & Museum Commission; Records of the Office of the Comptroller General, RG-4; Tax & Exoneration Lists, 1762-1794; Microfilm Roll: 329 In Pennsylvania archives, second series, Publication date 1896, in RETURNS AND ASSESSMENTS. COUNTY OF LANCASTER—1711

Portrait and Biographical Album of Ogle County, Illinois, Chicago, Chapman Brothers, 1886,

Rupp, Israel Daniel. A Collection of upwards of THIRTY THOUSAND NAMES of German, Swiss, Dutch, French and other   Immigrants in Pennsylvania from 1727 to 1776, Baltimore Genealogical Publishing Co., 1965

Rupp, Israel Daniel. History of Lancaster County: To which is Prefixed a Brief Sketch of the History of Pennsylvania. Gerlbert Hills Publisher, 1884

Towsley, Genevieve, "Skylines" in Naperville Sun, Jan 20, 1982

Van Kirk, Susie, Fort Humboldt Conflict Period [items from the Humboldt Times]

Welch, Charles Howard History of Mount Union, Shirleysburg and Shirley Township

Wells, Harry Laurenz. History of Siskiyou County, California Illustrated with Views of Residences, Business Buildings and Natural Scenery: And Containing Portraits and Biographies of Its Leading Citizens and Pioneers. D. J. Steward & Co., Oakland, California. 1881. Siskiyou Historical Society, 1881 - Siskiyou County (Calif.).

Wolz, Flora Lee, The Wolz Family

Wood, Doris. A SMALL TOWN WEATHERS THE DEPRESSION Naperville, Illinois, 1929-39, 1972

Internet

http://awiatsea.com
http://www.colonialsense.com/Society-Lifestyle/Signs_of_the_Times/Conestoga_Wagon/Wagon_Makers.php
https://commons.m.wikimedia.org/wiki/Category:U.S._Army_Base_Hospital_No._13
http://en.wikipedia.org/wiki/Samuel_Fuller_(Pilgrim)
http://familysearch.org
http://freepages.genealogy.rootsweb.ancestry.com/~jdavis/b1171.htm
http://nahc.ca.gov/webmaster/atlas/evidence/i0392.pdf
http://ogle.illinoisgenweb.org/PineCreekBrethren.txt
http://www.cyberbee.com/primary/Letter/investigation_sites.html
http://www.latta.org/Branches/Branch%2017.htm
http://library.mysticseaport.org/initiative/SalemSelect.cfm
http://www.myheritage.com/names/john_grush
http://www.myheritage.com/site-139915081/green
http://www.mytrees.com/newanc/Germany/Born-1715/Gr/Grush-family/Joseph-Grush-ry000196-660.htm
http://ogle.illinoisgenweb.org/PineCreekBrethren.txt
http://www.rootsweb.ancestry.com/~iabiog/poweshiek/hp1880/deeriver-dh.htm
http://www.saintandrewschurch.net/jane-behrel
https://www.theshipslist.com/ships/passengerlists/Forty-Niners.shtml
http://www.zentmeyergenealogy.com/germany.html
https://www.lancastercountymag.com/lititz-keeping-history-alive/

https://www.lititzmoravian.org/about-us/
https://www.oglecountyhistoricalsociety.com/
https://www.warwicktownship.org/administration/pages/history-of-the-township
Paper Trails (http://www.paper-trail.org/), a searchable website of diaries, letters and other documents pertaining to the overland travels of pioneers to Oregon, California, Utah and Montana in the 19th century, put together by the Oregon-California Trails Association
The Ranks of the Rancks (on-line edition, 10/19/2011), Ranck Family Heritage Society, Inc., http://Ranck.o

Newspapers

Democratic Standard, Hollidaysburg, Pa., Wednesday, January 28, 1863
Chicago Suburban Daily Herald on December 18, 2002
Chicago Tribune
Daily Alta California, Volume 10, Number 177, 29 June 1858
Freeport Journal-Standard, Freeport, Illinois, June 16, 1948, Page 11
Humboldt Times, various, 1854 and 1858
Naperville Events
Naperville Sun
Nevada Journal, Volume 3, Number 49, 31 March 1854, October 05, 1860
Ogle County Press, Saturday, January 2nd, 1886
Sacramento Daily Union, 24 June 1858, January 2, 1865, Page 6
Tri-County Press, Polo, Illinois, Thursday, May 8th, 1924